WORLD CUP

2006

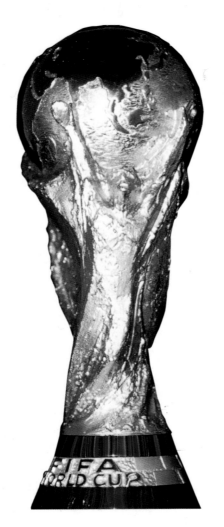

SELECT
EDITIONS

NEIL MARTIN

This edition published by Selectabook 2006

Folly Road,
Roundway,
Devizes,
Wiltshire,
SN10 2HT

Email: selectabookltd@tiscali.co.uk

Copyright ©2006 Taj Books Ltd
reprinted in 2006

All notations of errors or omissions (author inquiries, permissions) concerning the content of this book should be addressed to TAJ Books 27, Ferndown Gardens, Cobham, Surrey, UK, KT11 2BH, info@tajbooks.com.

ISBN (10) 1-84406-070-5
ISBN (13) 978-1-84406-070-2

Printed in China.
1 2 3 4 5 09 08 07 06

CONTENTS

A GROUP OF visionary French football administrators, led in the 1920s by the innovative Jules Rimet, are credited with the original idea of bringing the world's strongest national football teams together to compete for the title of World Champions. The original gold trophy bore Jules Rimet's name and was contested three times in the 1930s, before the Second World War put a 12-year stop to the competition.

When it resumed, the FIFA World Cup rapidly advanced to its undisputed status as the greatest single sporting event of the modern world. Held since 1958 alternately in Europe and the Americas, the World Cup broke new ground with the Executive Committee's decision in May 1996 to select Korea and Japan as co-hosts for the 2002 edition. FIFA's (Fédération Internationale de Football Association) flagship has constantly grown in popularity

and prestige

The world cup is the world's biggest sports event – with more than 1 billion people watching the 2002 Final between Brazil and Germany on TV.

A cumulative 44 billion are expected to tune in for the month-long tournament in Germany, with coverage beamed to 213 countries across the globe.

That is the attraction of watching the world's best players vying for the most coveted trophy in football.

Only seven nations have been skilful enough to claim the title, with Brazil – five times winners - the dominant force since the tournament came into existence in 1930. Uruguay (1930,1950), Argentina (1978, 1986), Italy (1934, 1938, 1982), West Germany (1954, 1974, 1990), France (1998) and England (1966) are the other previous winners.

Like Mexico, Italy and France, Germany is now organising its second FIFA World Cup. The first saw the great Franz Beckenbauer lift the trophy as captain of the winning team. Today, he presides over the Local Organising Committee in the run-up to a tournament which has changed considerably down the years: back in 1974, only sixteen sides took part, including the now-defunct German Democratic Republic (GDR) and Zaire. The latter were the only representative from the African continent and conceded fourteen goals with no reply.

TOP LEFT: *Jules Rimet - FIFA President 1921 to 1954 and namesake of the Original World Cup Trophy*

TOP: *On 8 June 1998 Joseph S. Blatter (Switzerland) was elected as the successor to Dr. João Havelange (Brazil) as the eighth FIFA President. This victory at the 51st FIFA Ordinary Congress in Paris (France) elevated Joseph S. Blatter, who had already served FIFA in various positions for twenty-three years, onto the highest rang in international football.*

RIGHT: *FIFA World Cup Trophy - With the Jules Rimet Cup now in the permanent possession of Brazil after their third World Cup triumph in Mexico City in 1970, FIFA commissioned a new trophy for the tenth World Cup in 1974. A total of 53 designs were submitted to FIFA by experts from seven countries, with the final choice being the work of Italian artist Silvio Gazzaniga.*

FAR LEFT: *The Jules Rimet Trophy - The original trophy was 35cm high and weighed approximately 3.8 kg. The statuette was made of sterling silver and gold plated, with a blue base made of semi-precious stone (lapis lazuli).*

Competition is sure to be fierce again in Germany with more than 700 players involved in 64 matches in 12 state-of-the-art stadiums. Attendance figures will top more than 3 million alone.

It has taken 18 months of qualifying to whittle it down to 32 Finalists, with a total of 847 games being played across six continents.

And of the lucky 32 there will be some new faces at the World Cup this year. Angola, Togo, Ivory Coast, Ghana, Ukraine and Trinidad and Tobago are all making their first appearance – taking the all-time figure to 79 nations who have competed in the Finals.

Holders Brazil are expected to start as favourites to lift the trophy yet again in Berlin on July 9, but Argentina, France, Italy, Holland and England have also been tipped to go all the way.

Host nations have fared well over the years winning the 1930, 1934, 1966, 1974, 1978 and 1998 World Cups.

History shows that a little bit of luck is often needed by the triumphant team and a global population waits to see who fortune favours at the 18th World Cup.

ABOVE: *England Manager Sir Alf Ramsey - "We will win the World Cup," the Essex man announced with uncharacteristic bravado as he took the national team reins in 1963.*

LEFT: *Ferenc Puskas - Hungary's finest ever player and one of the greatest footballers ever to grace the FIFA World Cup, Ferenc Puskas was the figurehead of the ground breaking Hungary team that dominated world football in the early 1950s.*

The FIFA World Cup has also been punctuated by dramatic upsets that have helped create footballing history - the United States defeating England in 1950, North Korea's defeat of Italy in 1966, Cameroon's emergence in the 1980s, their opening match defeat of the Argentinean cup-holders in 1990 and in 2002 holders France were eliminated without even scoring a goal...

ABOVE: *Pele - "I was born for soccer, just as Beethoven was born for music." Arrogant, pompous words. Except when they are spoken by Edson Arantes do Nascimento, the Brazilian genius known throughout the football world as Pele. A veteran of four World Cups, scorer of 1,283 first-class goals - 12 of them in World Cup final tournaments - a member of those magical Brazilian squads that won soccer's greatest prize in 1958, 1962 and 1970.*

ABOVE: *Diego Armando Maradona - Undoubtedly Argentinas finest player however his talent is overshadowed by his tendency to cheat and his repeated drug abuse.*

LEFT: *Uruguay on their way to beating Argentina 4-2 in the first World Cup Final in the Centenario stadium, Montevideo in front of a crowd of 80,000.*

THE WORLD cup was born in 1930 following two successful football tournaments at the Olympic Games – both of which were won by Uruguay. Therefore, when FIFA held a vote in 1929 to decide the hosts for their inaugural international tournament, Uruguay were the obvious choice despite the distance European teams would have to travel. Two months before the competition started, no representatives from Europe had agreed to make the long trip which promised to be long, tiring and costly. Thus, more and more European associations broke their promise to participate., but after a personal intervention by FIFA president Jules Rimet four countries – Belgium, France, Romania and Yugoslavia – agreed to share a ship across the Atlantic. They set sail on 21 June 1930 from Villefranche-Sur-Mer with the liner "Conte Verde" reaching Rio de Janeiro on 29 June, picking up the Brazilian squad on the way before landing in Montevideo on 4 July, nine days before the first match. The tournament eventually included 13 teams – the four Europeans joined by eight from South America and a representative line-up from USA – split into four groups. Argentina and Uruguay looked the early favourites as they qualified with 100 per cent records, the surprise of the tournament came from USA and Yugoslavia who joined them in the semi-finals after knocking out the likes of Brazil and Romania – coached by King Carol. Europe did very well as typified by the French team, beating Mexico 4 - 1 and going down narrowly to Argentina 1 - 0 in an epic struggle. The referee, who had blown the final whistle six minutes early, finally - after fierce protests - recalled the players to the field, some of whom were already in the shower! However, Argentina and Uruguay were easy winners as they both cruised to 6-1 victories in the semi-finals to set up a mouth-watering finale in the 100,000-seater Centenario Stadium. The rivalry began before the Final even kicked off, as a row over the ball to be used ensured that Argentina provided their own for the first-half, before a switch to one from Uruguay after the break. Whether that had any effect is unclear, but Argentina were 2-1 up at half-time before the home side came storming back to claim the first trophy – the 30cm high Victoire aux Ailes d'Or – with a 4-2 win.

DATE	LOCATION	TEAMS	FULL/(HALF) TIME SCORE	VENUE
SEMI-FINALS				
27-JUL-30	MONTEVIDEO	Uruguay:Yugoslavia	6:1 (3:1)	Centenario
26-JUL-30	MONTEVIDEO	Argentina:USA	6:1 (1:0)	Centenario
FINAL				
30-JUL-30	MONTEVIDEO	Uruguay:Argentina	4:2 (1:2)	Centenario

ABOVE: *The victorious Italian team who beat Czechoslovakia in the final with goals from Orsi and Schiavio for Italy and one from Puc for the Czechs.*

HOME-FIELD ADVANTAGE once again proved vital as Italy claimed the first World Cup played on European soil. The tournament was dominated by European teams as Brazil and Argentina sent severely under-strength sides and ended up making the 7,000-mile trip home after just one game each. Meanwhile, Uruguay did not even travel as they turned down the chance to defend their title, but Italy came through the qualification process to stake their claims in front of an expectant nation. They possessed a talented squad, but rumours swirled that referees were being pressurised by Italian Prime Minister Benito Mussolini to favour the home team and suspicion was further aroused when Swede Ivan Eklind was chosen to officiate both their semi-final and the Final itself. Italy played Austria in the semi, having won the first ever World Cup replay against Spain in the previous round, and won through thanks to an early goal from Enrico Guaita. Czechoslovakia, meanwhile, won three tight games against Romania, Switzerland and Germany to set up an eagerly-awaited Final in Rome, with the overwhelming majority of the 50,000 fans inside the stadium wearing blue. Both sides looked drained as they played their fourth game in just over a week, but the frenzied home crowd were then silenced when the Czechs took the lead on 76 minutes through Antonin Puc. Italy were not prepared to let the trophy slip through their grasp, though, and dug deep to score an equaliser before Angelo Schiavio netted the winner in extra-time.

DATE	LOCATION	TEAMS	FULL/(HALF) TIME SCORE	VENUE
SEMI-FINALS				
03-JUN-34	MILAN	Italy:Austria	1:0 (1:0)	San Siro
03-JUN-34	ROME	Czechoslovakia:Germany	3:1 (1:0)	Nazionale PNF
MATCH FOR 3RD PLACE				
07-JUN-34	NAPLES	Germany:Austria	3:2 (3:1)	Giorgio Ascarelli
FINAL				
10-JUN-34	ROME	Italy:Czechoslovakia	2:1 a.e.t (1:1, 0:0)	Nazionale PNF

ABOVE: *The World Cup holders, Italy retain their trophy with a 4-2 win over Hungary with two goals a piece for the Italians Colaussi and Piola, with Hungarian goals from Titkos and Sarosi.*

THE THIRD World Cup Finals were played in France under the shadow of impending war clouds that ultimately robbed the tournament of a number of top teams. Argentina and Uruguay both refused to travel from South America, while Spain was being ravaged by a civil war and Austria was ruled out having been annexed by Hitler's Germany. The hosts were given automatic entry – a privilege that still survives – and rebuilt a number of stadiums to put on a good show, but could only reach the quarter-finals. England were again absent after a disagreement with FIFA over payments to amateur players, but Brazil did make the journey and immediately set the tournament alight. Star striker Leonidas netted four goals in an amazing 6-5 win over Poland in the first round, while Ernest Wilimowski could feel somewhat unfortunate having scored the same number for the defeated Poles. The Brazilians then beat Czechoslovakia in the quarter-finals after a replay, but their coach Adheniar Pimenta then made a critical error in resting Leonidas for the semi-final – obviously confident they would be playing another game – which allowed title holders Italy to grab a 2-1 win. In the Final, the Italians faced Hungary who had conceded just one goal in three games up to that stage. However, Italy took control thanks to playmakers Giuseppe Meazza and Giovanni Ferrari, while Silvio Piola scored twice in a 4-2 victory that ensured the Azzurri claimed back-to-back victories, although the resulting war robbed the 1938 squad of the chance of making it three in a row.

DATE	LOCATION	TEAMS	FULL/(HALF) TIME SCORE	VENUE
SEMI-FINALS				
16-JUN-38	MARSEILLES	Italy:Brazil	2:1 (0:0)	Velodrome
16-JUN-38	PARIS	Hungary:Sweden	5:1 (3:1)	Parc des Princes
MATCH FOR 3RD PLACE				
19-JUN-38	BORDEAUX	Brazil:Sweden	4:2 (1:2)	Parc Lescure
FINAL				
19-JUN-38	COLOMBES-PARIS	Italy:Hungary	4:2 (3:1)	Olympique

ABOVE: *Jackie Milburn heads the ball towards the Spanish goal during England's 1-0 defeat to Spain in Rio de Janeiro. Following their shock defeat 3 days earlier by the USA.*

THE WORLD cup returned after a 12-year absence due to the war and featured the most bizarre ever 'Final'. The famous trophy, which had been kept hidden in a shoe-box underneath the bed of the vice-President of FIFA while hostilities raged across Europe, was again up for grabs – with the Brazilian hosts desperate to claim victory. With only 13 countries competing, FIFA opted for a strange two-group system which saw Uruguay reach the final stages by winning just one match – a comprehensive 8-0 win over Bolivia. England made a good start to their first-ever campaign with a 2-0 win over Chile, but despite a star-studded line-up for the age that included Tom Finney, Billy Wright, Stan Mortensen and Wilf Mannion they were stunned 1-0 by USA. Such was the shock that the team failed to recover their composure and lost 1-0 in their next match against Spain when a win would have put them through. Brazil, which had seen a massive boom in the popularity in football following their impact on the 1938 tournament, were cheered on by passionate supporters at their new cavernous stadium – the Maracana. More than 140,000 turned up for the first round clash with Yugoslavia that secured the home side's place in the final stages. They looked odds-on to lift the trophy after thrashing Sweden 7-1 and Spain 6-1 in their first two games of the four-team group that decided the champions, but in their final match – despite 174,000 fans behind them – they let an early lead against Uruguay slip and Alcides Ghiggia netted with 11 minutes remaining to secure a second world title for their South American rivals.

TEAM	RANK	P	W	D	L	GF	GA	PTS
URUGUAY	1	3	2	1	0	7	5	7
BRAZIL	2	3	2	0	1	14	4	6
SWEDEN	3	3	1	0	2	6	11	3
SPAIN	4	3	0	1	2	4	11	1

ABOVE: *Germany inside-right., Max Morlock shoots his side's first goal past Hungarian goalkeeper, Gyula Grosits, with Hungary left-back, Mihaly Lantos between them.*

LEFT: *German captain, Fritz Walter with the Jules Rimet gold trophy at Bern, July 4th, after his team had beaten the favoured Hungarians 3-2 in the world cup final.*

URUGUAY WENT into the 1954 World Cup with an enviable record – two time winners from their previous two tournaments and still unbeaten in the competition. That record looked set to be extended as the South Americans marched to the semi-finals, only to be stopped in their tracks by an emerging Hungarian side that quickly became known as the Magical Magyars. With the likes of Ferenc Puskas, Sandor Kocsis and Jozsef Bozsik, Hungary smashed Korea 9-0 and West Germany 8-3 in the group stage before shocking Brazil 4-2 in the quarter-finals in a game that was over-shadowed by an amazing fight between the players in the dressing rooms after the final whistle. They needed extra-time to finally beat Uruguay, but the eventual 4-2 win made them the hot favourites for the Final. Elsewhere, the goals were flying in and the final tally was a staggering 140 in 26 games for an average of 5.38 per game. England got in on the act with a 4-4 draw against Belgium to qualify for the quarter-finals, but they were then sent home by Uruguay. In the other half of the draw, West Germany regrouped and claimed a place in the Final thanks to wins over Yugoslavia and Austria in the knock-out stages, but they were rank outsiders given their hammering at the hands of Hungary earlier in the tournament. It did not look for the Germans when they went 2-0 down within eight minutes, but they battled back and Helmut Rahn netted the winner with just six minutes remaining as Hungarian goalkeeper Gyula Grosics slipped on the slippery turf.

DATE	LOCATION	TEAMS	FULL/(HALF) TIME SCORE	VENUE
SEMI-FINALS				
30-JUN-54	BASEL	Germany FR:Austria	6:1 (1:0)	St. Jakob
30-JUN-54	LAUSANNE	Hungary:Uruguay	4:2 a.e.t (2:2, 1:0)	La Pontaise
MATCH FOR 3RD PLACE				
03-JUL-54	ZURICH	Austria:Uruguay	3:1 (1:1)	Hardturm
FINAL				
04-JUL-54	BERNE	Germany FR:Hungary	3:2 (2:2)	Wankdorf

ABOVE: *President of Brazil Dr Jusoelino Kubitschek toasts the Brazilian football team for bringing home the Rimet Cup as the new World Champions at soccer.*

TOP: *Just Fontaine of France is carried by his team mates after scoring four goals against West Germany and becoming the World Cup top scorer with thirteen goals.*

ABOVE: *Seventeen year old Pele weeps on the shoulder of team-mate Didi as Garrincha and Orlando (right) comfort him, after Brazil had won 5-2 in the World Cup final.*

BRAZIL CLAIMED their first World Cup as a previously unknown 17-year called Pele burst onto the scene. He arrived in Sweden with an injury and was held back until the third group game, but was virtually unstoppable after that as he scored the winner over Wales in the quarter-finals, a hat-trick against France in the semi and another two as the hosts were swept aside in the Final. Despite all that, the new star was a long way from winning the Golden Boot as Just Fontaine hit an incredible 13 goals for a French team determined to attack. They netted 17 goals in just five games, but were ultimately thwarted by Brazil. There was plenty of interest for the Home Nations with England, Wales, Scotland and Northern Ireland all involved. Scotland finished bottom of their group, while the other three all ended up in play-offs to qualify from their respective groups. Wales and Northern Ireland were successful, but England lost to the USSR. Wales did well to restrict Brazil and Pele to just one goal in the quarter-final while Northern Ireland were swept aside 4-0 by Fontaine and France at the same stage. In the mean time, hosts Sweden made their way quietly to the Final by beating USSR and West Germany, but even with around 50,000 supporters cheering them on against Brazil with the trophy at stake, they were no match for the South Americans as Pele helped them to a 5-2 victory.

DATE	LOCATION	TEAMS	FULL/(HALF) TIME SCORE	VENUE
SEMI-FINALS				
24-JUN-58	GOTHENBURG	Sweden:Germany FR	3:1 (1:1)	Nya Ullevi
24-JUN-58	STOCKHOLM	Brazil:France	5:2 (2:1)	Rasunda
MATCH FOR 3RD PLACE				
28-JUN-58	GOTHENBURG	France:Germany FR	6:3 (3:1)	Nya Ullevi
FINAL				
29-JUN-58	STOCKHOLM	Brazil:Sweden	5:2 (2:1)	Rasunda

ABOVE: *Brazilian soccer star Pele, unable to play in the World Cup final because of injuries sustained in an earlier tie, hugs his replacement Amarildo.*

TOP RIGHT: *Police and referee Ashton escort Italian player Ferrini from the field after heated quarrels broke out between players of the two teams.*

RIGHT: *Vava of Brazil celebrates after he scores the third goal as Brazil defeat Czechoslovakia 3-1 to win the World Cup.*

BRAZIL CLAIMED their second successive World Cup, but the tournament was overshadowed by some violent encounters. Pele, who had burst onto the scene four years earlier in Sweden, was immediately targeted for some rough challenges and his tournament was over when he suffered a torn muscle in only the second game against Czechoslovakia. Worse was to come, however, when Italy and Chile were involved in a lawless encounter that was quickly dubbed the Battle of Santiago. Italy's Giorgio Ferrini was sent off inside eight minutes, before Chilean Leonel Sanchez somehow avoided punishment for a blatant punch which floored Mario David. The Italian later got his own retribution, and a red card, for a flying karate kick on Sanchez as the game descended into turmoil. England, meanwhile, overcame an opening game defeat to Hungary to qualify for the quarter-finals thanks to a 3-1 win over Argentina and a 0-0 draw with Bulgaria. However, Brazil ended their run in the next match as Garrincha inspired the South Americans to a 3-1 victory to send Walter Winterbottom's side home, before hosts Chile were despatched at the semi-final stage to secure another tilt at the title. In the other half of the draw, surprise package Czechoslovakia beat the much-fancied Hungarians and then claimed a place in the Final with a 3-1 win over Yugoslavia. The Czechs even took a shock lead in the Final but Amarildo - the replacement for Pele - quickly equalised and Zito and Vava added further goals to ensure the Brazilians held onto their title of world champions.

DATE	LOCATION	TEAMS	FULL/(HALF) TIME SCORE	VENUE
SEMI-FINALS				
13-JUN-62	SANTIAGO	Brazil:Chile	4:2 (2:1)	Nacional
13-JUN-62	VINA DEL MAR	Czechoslovakia:Yugoslavia	3:1 (0:0)	Sausalito
MATCH FOR 3RD PLACE				
16-JUN-62	SANTIAGO	Chile:Yugoslavia	1:0 (0:0)	Nacional
FINAL				
17-JUN-62	SANTIAGO	Brazil:Czechoslovakia	3:1 (1:1)	Nacional

ABOVE: *England's Geoff Hurst scores the fourth goal to complete a historic hat-trick*

TOP RIGHT: *Back Row (L-R): Manager Alf Ramsey, Ray Wilson, George Cohen, Jack Charlton, Gordon Banks, Roger Hunt, Nobby Stiles, Assistant Manager Harold Sheperdson. Front Row (L-R): Bobby Charlton, Alan Ball, Bobby Moore, Geoff Hurst and Martin Peters*

RIGHT: *England captain Bobby Moore on shoulders of teammates holding aloft the Jules Rimet trophy.*

GEOFF HURST etched his name in England folklore as the Three Lions enjoyed their greatest ever triumph. The West Ham striker netted a hat-trick – including one of the most debatable goals in international history – to help sink West Germany 4-2 in the Final and cap a perfect tournament for the hosts. However, Brazil were the favourites when the competition began having won the previous two World Cups. But Pele, just as he had been four years earlier in Chile, was once again targeted by over-physical Bulgarian and Portuguese defenders and the title-holders were surprisingly eliminated at the group stage. Another shock failure came from the Italians as they lost 1-0 to North Korea at Ayresome Park to force them to return home before the knock-out stages. The Koreans then threatened another stunning result in the quarter-finals as they raced into a 3-0 lead inside 25 minutes against Portugal, only for Eusebio to show his class with four goals to help his side record a 5-3 win. England, meanwhile, beat Argentina 1-0 despite a furore over Antonio Rattin's first-half red card and then had Bobby Charlton to thank for the two goals that helped secure a 2-1 win over the Portuguese in the semi-final. That set up a mouthwatering clash with West Germany at Wembley on July 30 and the match did not disappoint. The Germans took an early lead, but goals from Hurst and Martin Peters looked set to secure the victory. However, Wolfgang Weber's last-gasp equaliser took the game to extra-time. Arguments still rage as to whether Hurst's second goal actually crossed the line, but his third was emphatic as England claimed the World Cup for the first time.

DATE	LOCATION	TEAMS	FULL/(HALF) TIME SCORE	VENUE
SEMI-FINALS				
26-JUL-66	LONDON	England:Portugal	2:1 (1:0)	Wembley
25-JUL-66	LIVERPOOL	Germany FR:Soviet Union	2:1 (1:0)	Goodison Park
MATCH FOR 3RD PLACE				
28-JUL-66	LONDON	Portugal *v* Soviet Union	2:1 (1:1)	Wembley
FINAL				
30-JUL-66	LONDON	England *v* Germany FR	4:2 a.e.t (2:2, 1:1)	Wembley

ABOVE: *England's Bobby Moore swapping shirts with Pele.*

LEFT: *England's Gordon Banks makes an incredible save from Brazil's Pele.*

TOP: *Brazil's Pele celebrates after scoring the opening goal in the final against Italy. His fourth of the tournament.*

BRAZIL CAPPED probably the best-ever World Cup by claiming the title for the third time – and therefore keeping the trophy for good. In a festival of football, the Brazilians dazzled the brightest with 19 goals in just six matches as they won every single match on the road to glory. Holders England looked on course for another decent showing as they led 2-0 with just 20 minutes remaining of their quarter-final against West Germany. However, influential midfielder Bobby Charlton was then substituted to ensure he had fresh legs for the apparent semi-final – only for the Germans to hit back and win the game 3-2 in extra-time. It was a cruel way to go out, especially for skipper Bobby Moore who had performed so valiantly – not least in the group game against Brazil when Pele had singled him out at the final whistle to exchange shirts in one of the most famous images of the tournament. Germany went on to face Italy in a semi-final that is widely regarded as one of the best ever. Karl-Heinz Schnellinger scored a last minute equaliser to keep the Germans in it and they then went ahead in extra-time, but were ultimately beaten 4-3 in a real thriller. Italy appeared exhausted in the Final as Brazil danced across the pitch, most famously for their fourth goal in the 4-1 victory which culminated in Jairzinho cracking the ball into the net and maintaining his own amazing record of scoring in every match of the competition.

DATE	LOCATION	TEAMS	FULL/(HALF) TIME SCORE	VENUE
SEMI-FINALS				
17-JUN-70	MEXICO CITY	Italy:Germany FR	4:3 a.e.t (1:1, 1:0)	Azteca
17-JUN-70	GUADALAJARA	Brazil:Uruguay	3:1 (1:1)	Jalisco
MATCH FOR 3RD PLACE				
20-JUN-70	MEXICO CITY	Germany FR:Uruguay	1:0 (1:0)	Azteca
FINAL				
21-JUN-70	MEXICO CITY	Brazil:Italy	4:1 (1:1)	Azteca

ABOVE: *Johan Cruyff of Holland. Only played in one FIFA World Cup, but his skills made him an instant superstar.*

ABOVE: *West Germany Captain Franz Beckenbauer ("Emperor Franz" and "The Kaiser" the fans called him) lifts the World Cup trophy.*

GERMAN EFFICIENCY overcame 'Total Football' from Holland as the host nation claimed the trophy for the first time since 1954. With the Jules Rimet trophy retired following Brazil's third triumph in 1970, a new piece of gold – sculpted by Silvio Gazzaniga - was up for grabs. Unfortunately for England, they had no chance of lifting it after a 1-1 draw at home to Poland in qualifying ensured they would not be making the trip to Germany. The Poles, however, grabbed the opportunity and propelled by seven goals from eventual Golden Boot winner Gzregorz Lato they claimed the notable scalps of Argentina and Italy before their dreams of reaching the Final were quashed by the hosts in the last game of the second group stage. The final was contended by the winners of group A and the winners of Group B, thus doing away with the semi-finals. The stars of the tournament, though, were undoubtedly the Dutch as Johan Cruyff – who unveiled his trademark turn to a mesmerised audience - Johan Neeskens and Jonny Rep produced a thrilling brand of football that swept aside the likes of Uruguay, Argentina and holders Brazil on their way to the Final. And they made a stunning start once they got there, with English referee Jack Taylor risking the wrath of the home crowd by awarding Holland a penalty – converted by Neeskens – in the first minute before Germany had even touched the ball. However, the Germans tightened up – most notably with man-marker Berti Vogts – and then turned the match around with goals from Paul Breitner and Gerd Muller to claim the victory.

DATE	LOCATION	TEAMS	FULL/(HALF) TIME SCORE	VENUE
MATCH FOR 3RD PLACE				
06-JUL-74	MUNICH	Brazil:Poland	0:1 (0:0)	Olympiastadion
FINAL				
07-JUL-74	MUNICH	Netherlands:Germany FR	1:2 (1:2)	Olympiastadion

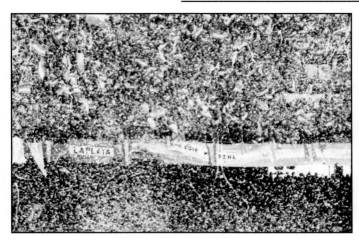

ABOVE: *Ticker tape is thrown by Argentina fans.*

TOP RIGHT: *Argentina's Mario Kempes top scorer in the tournament with six goals.*

RIGHT: *Argentina's Daniel Passarella with the World Cup trophy.*

ARGENTINA PUT on a great show before claiming the trophy for the first time in their history. The South Americans had featured in the first ever Final back in 1930 – when they were beaten by Uruguay – so it ended a long 48 year wait for glory. England failed to feature in tournament yet again, despite only losing one game in qualifying, so Scotland carried the British flag. However, a shock defeat to Peru and a draw against Iran left them needing a four-goal win over Holland to progress, so the resulting 3-2 victory was ultimately in vain. Holland squeezed through, therefore, but then hit top gear in the second group stage as the likes of Johann Neeskens and Jonny Rep helped them power past Italy and West Germany to qualify for the Final. Hosts Argentina, meanwhile, had also started slowly and they were in danger of missing out on a place in the Final to arch-rivals Brazil as they went into their last game of the second group stage needing to beat Peru by four clear goals, to qualify for the final on goal difference. Mario Kempes was on fire and scored twice as the Peruvians were thrashed 6-0 to set up a mouthwatering clash with the Dutch. Holland, without Johann Cruyff who had refused to travel in protest at General Videla's totalitarian regime in Argentina, battled bravely as more than 71,000 locals roared on their heroes – but they went down 3-1 in extra-time to lose their second successive Final. Kempes scored two more to finish as Golden Boot winner with six and captain Daniel Passarella was able to lift the trophy on home soil.

Date	Location	Teams	Full/(Half) Time Score	Venue
Match for 3rd place				
24-JUN-78	BUENOS AIRES	Brazil:Italy	2:1 (0:1)	River Plate
Final				
25-JUN-78	BUENOS AIRES	Argentina:Netherlands	3:1 a.e.t (1:1, 1:0)	River Plate

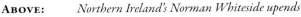

ABOVE: *Northern Ireland's Norman Whiteside upends Austria's Bernd Krauss.*

TOP RIGHT: *Paolo Rossi scores for Italy and wins the Golden Boot with Six goals scored.*

RIGHT: *Italy's Dino Zoff lifts the World Cup trophy. He became the Oldest Captain ever to win the World Cup.*

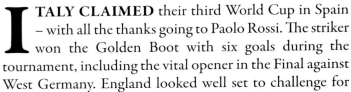

ITALY CLAIMED their third World Cup in Spain – with all the thanks going to Paolo Rossi. The striker won the Golden Boot with six goals during the tournament, including the vital opener in the Final against West Germany. England looked well set to challenge for the title after winning their opening group with a 100 per cent record, including a goal for Bryan Robson against France in an incredible 27 seconds. However, two goalless draws against West Germany and Spain were not enough to put them through from the second group stage as they frustratingly went home unbeaten. Northern Ireland – who made Norman Whiteside the youngest ever World Cup player at the age of just 17 years and 42 days - also topped their opening group, before being knocked out with a 4-1 defeat to the impressive French, but Scotland lasted just three games. All that was an appetiser to the later action, though, as fans were treated to two of the all-time classic matches. First, the scintillating Brazilian team – featuring the likes of Zico, Socrates and Falcao – were scuppered by a 3-2 defeat to Italy in the second group stage as Rossi grabbed the headlines with a hat-trick. Then France and West Germany played out a thrilling semi-final that had it all, most notably one of the worst tackles ever seen. German goalkeeper Toni Schumacher left Patrick Battiston unconscious with an horrific foul that did not even draw a free-kick, let alone a booking. To add to France's frustrations, they ended up losing a sensational game on penalties having led 3-1 in extra-time. Germany were no match for the Italians in the Final, though, as they went down 3-1 in a one-sided encounter to give goalkeeper Dino Zoff the honour of lifting the cup.

DATE	LOCATION	TEAMS	FULL/(HALF) TIME SCORE	VENUE
SEMI-FINALS				
08-JUL-82	SEVILLE	Germany FR:France	3:3 a.e.t (1:1, 1:1) 5:4 PSO	Sanchez Pizjuan
08-JUL-82	BARCELONA	Poland:Italy	0:2 (0:1)	Camp Nou
MATCH FOR 3RD PLACE				
10-JUL-82	ALICANTE	Poland:France	3:2 (2:1)	Jose Rico Perez
FINAL				
11-JUL-82	MADRID	Italy:Germany FR	3:1 (0:0)	Santiago Bernabeu

ABOVE: *Argentina's Diego Maradona beats England's Peter Shilton to the ball to score the first goal with his hand, which became known as the Hand of God.*

TOP RIGHT: *West Germany's Rudi Voller scores the second goal to equalise.*

RIGHT: *Argentina's Diego Maradona lifts the World Cup trophy.*

DIEGO MARADONA was the undoubted star in Mexico as he virtually single-handedly steered Argentina to World Cup glory. The midfield maestro scored two of the best goals ever seen at the tournament, but also grabbed the headlines for all the wrong reasons in one of the most blatant acts of cheating. Maradona's second effort against England in the quarter-finals was simply sublime as he weaved his way through the defence, but what had gone before it was scandalous as he blatantly punched Argentina with front in a goal he later attributed to the 'Hand of God'. It was cruel end for England after they had picked up momentum following a shaky start, thanks largely to the predatory instincts of Gary Lineker – who still finished the tournament as Golden Boot winner with six goals. Elsewhere for the Home Nations, Northern Ireland were unfortunate to be drawn in a group containing Spain and Brazil, while Scotland lost to Denmark and West Germany to return home early as well. France were widely expected to face Maradona in the Final as they beat Italy and Brazil thanks to the brilliant midfield of Michel Platini, Jean Tigana and Alain Giresse. However, their run came to an end for the second successive time against the Germans in the semi-final. Maradona, who had netted his second stunning goal against Belgium in the semi-finals, was not on the scoresheet in the Final – but he was undoubtedly the inspiration behind the 3-2 victory over West Germany to spark wild scenes in South America.

DATE	LOCATION	TEAMS	FULL/(HALF) TIME SCORE	VENUE
SEMI-FINALS				
25-JUN-86	MEXICO CITY	Argentina:Belgium	2:0 (0:0)	Azteca
25-JUN-86	GUADALAJARA	France:Germany FR	0:2 (0:1)	Jalisco
MATCH FOR 3RD PLACE				
28-JUN-86	PUEBLA	France:Belgium	4:2 a.e.t (2:2, 2:1)	Cuauhtemoc
FINAL				
29-JUN-86	MEXICO CITY	Argentina:Germany FR	3:2 (1:0)	Azteca

ABOVE: *Germany's Jurgen Klinsmann is fouled by Argentina's Oscar Ruggeri.*

TOP RIGHT: *Argentina's Gustavo Dezotti is shown the red card and sent off by referee Edgardo Codesal Mendez.*

RIGHT: *West Germany's Andreas Brehme and Lothar Matthaus celebrate with the trophy.*

ENGLAND FANS might not have realised it, but this tournament was viewed as something of a let-down by the football world in general. While Three Lions supporters were caught up with the excitement of reaching the semi-finals, elsewhere the games failed to live up to the hype. The opening game was a cracker, though, as holders Argentina lost to underdogs Cameroon despite the Africans having two players sent off. While Cameroon continued to entertain, thanks largely to veteran striker Roger Milla, Scotland struggled again with their list of embarrassing World Cup results extended to include a 1-0 defeat to Costa Rica. Republic of Ireland caught the eye as they progressed to the knockout stages alongside England, then beat Romania in a dramatic penalty shoot-out before losing to Italy. All that was a cameo for England fans, however, as they were treated to a roller-coaster ride by Bobby Robson's side. A nervy group stage was followed by a last-gasp winner from David Platt over Belgium, before plucky Cameroon were finally despatched 3-2. That set up a semi-final showdown with arch-rivals Germany which ultimately led to heartbreak, and tears from Paul Gascoigne, following failure in the penalty shoot-out. Argentina, meanwhile, had regrouped and bored their way to the Final with a 1-0 win over an uncharacteristically unadventurous Brazilian side and two shoot-out wins over Yugoslavia and Italy. It was a penalty that decided the dour Final as well, with German defender Andreas Brehme holding his nerve in the 85th minute as Argentina's luck and discipline – Pedro Monzon and Gustavo Dezotti were both sent off – ran out.

DATE	LOCATION	TEAMS	FULL/(HALF) TIME SCORE	VENUE
SEMI-FINALS				
04-JUL-90	TURIN	Germany FR:England	1:1 a.e.t (1:1, 0:0) 4:3 PSO	Delle Alpi
03-JUL-90	NAPLES	Italy:Argentina	1:1 a.e.t (1:1, 1:0) 3:4 PSO	San Paolo
MATCH FOR 3RD PLACE				
07-JUL-90	BARI	Italy:England	2:1 (0:0)	Sant Nicola
FINAL				
08-JUL-90	ROME	Germany FR:Argentina	1:0 (0:0)	Olimpico

TOP LEFT: *Roberto Baggio (Italy) misses in the penalty shoot out which means Brazil win the world cup.*

LEFT: *Brazilian keeper Taffarel celebrates winning the World Cup as a disconsolate Roberto Baggio stands motionless after saying his spot-kick during the penalty shoot-out to hand Brazil the trophy.*

ABOVE: *Brazil captain Dunga leads his victorious team-mates on their lap of honour after winning the 1994 World Cup.*

BASKETBALL, BASEBALL and American Football were all temporarily pushed aside as FIFA took the World Cup to USA in an attempt to spread the game to a new untapped market. While the crowds were the highest of any FIFA World Cup during the tournament, the legacy has not been a boom in football in the States, despite some exciting games up until a disappointing Final. Home Nations interest was low - with England, Scotland, Wales and Northern Ireland all failing to appear for the tournament for the first time since 1938 – but the Republic of Ireland again provided plenty of enjoyment, not least with a 1-0 win over Italy in their opening game. Argentina looked menacing, before Diego Maradona failed a drugs test to send the camp into turmoil ahead of a shock 3-2 defeat to Romania in the last 16. A bigger tragedy hit Colombia when defender Andres Escobar was shot dead on his return to the country having unfortunately netted an own goal against USA that helped prevent the South Americans progress from the group stages. Brazil, meanwhile, looked irresistible on their way to the Final, not least in the game of the tournament when they survived a superb fight back from Holland to finally run out 3-2 winners. Italy were virtually a one-man team as Roberto Baggio netted late goals against Nigeria and Spain, before ending Bulgaria's amazing run at the semi-finals stage with two early efforts. Thus it came as a massive surprise that following a poor goalless encounter the pony-tailed striker was the man to miss the crucial spot kick in the first-ever penalty shoot-out in a Final, as Brazil lifted the trophy yet again.

DATE	LOCATION	TEAMS	FULL/(HALF) TIME SCORE	VENUE
SEMI-FINALS				
13-JUL-94	LOS ANGELES	Sweden:Brazil	0:1 (0:0)	Rose Bowl
13-JUL-94	NEW YORK/NEW JERSEY	Bulgaria:Italy	1:2 (1:2)	Giants Stadium
MATCH FOR 3RD PLACE				
16-JUL-94	LOS ANGELES	Sweden:Bulgaria	4:0 (4:0)	Rose Bowl
FINAL				
17-JUL-94	LOS ANGELES	Brazil:Italy	0:0 a.e.t (0:0) 3:2 PSO	Rose Bowl

ABOVE: *Zinedine Zidane - France scores first goal V Brazil.*

TOP RIGHT: *Zinedine Zidane heads in his & France's 2nd goal. This was the first game in the entire tournament that he had scored in.*

RIGHT: *France's Didier Deschamps lifts the World Cup with Laurent Blanc , Marcel Desailly , Zinedine Zidane and Robert Pires.*

VIVE LA France was the cry as the hosts became the sixth team to lift the trophy on home soil. A young French side – including the likes of Thierry Henry, David Trezeguet and Patrick Vieira – came of age in dramatic style on a night of high drama against Brazil in the Final. Before then, however, Les Blues had enjoyed an unspectacular run through the competition, while their major rivals took each other out. The perennial under-achievers Spain once again failed to get past the group stages after a shock opening defeat to Nigeria, but the rest of the big teams made it through. England looked dangerous, but their dreams came to an end against Argentina and there was little comfort to be taken from the fact that it was one of the best matches in World Cup history. In a game that had everything, Michael Owen announced himself on the world stage with a wonder-goal, both teams scored from the penalty spot in normal time, David Beckham was sent off, Sol Campbell had a last minute winner ruled out before Carlos Roa saved David Batty's penalty in the shoot-out to send the Argentinians through. While France needed extra-time to beat Paraguay and a penalty shoot-out to overcome Italy, Brazil looked in superb form to breeze past Chile and Denmark. However, the South Americans almost stumbled in the semi-finals when they needed a shoot-out to beat Holland, while Lilian Thuram set up France's biggest ever game with both goals in a 2-1 win over Croatia. The Final will be remembered as much for the rumours about the health of Brazil's star striker Ronaldo in the minutes immediately before kick-off as it will for France's eventual 3-0 win. But the home side were unconcerned as they sparked off a night of celebrations on the Champs Elysees.

DATE	LOCATION	TEAMS	FULL/(HALF) TIME SCORE	VENUE
SEMI-FINALS				
08-JUL-98	SAINT-DENIS	France:Croatia	2:1 (0:0)	Stade de France
07-JUL-98	MARSEILLES	Brazil:Netherlands	1:1 a.e.t (1:1, 0:0) 4:2 PSO	Velodrome
MATCH FOR 3RD PLACE				
11-JUL-98	PARIS	Netherlands:Croatia	1:2 (1:2)	Parc des Princes
FINAL				
12-JUL-98	SAINT-DENIS	Brazil:France	0:3 (0:2)	Stade de France

ASIA HOSTED its first ever World Cup – and Japan and South Korea were immediately gripped by football fever. The opening stages set the scene for a thrilling tournament as holders France were eliminated without even scoring a goal, while much-fancied Argentina and Portugal were also knocked-out at the group stages. The underdogs, meanwhile, were enjoying unparalleled success with Senegal, Turkey and USA all reaching the quarter-finals. They were joined by South Korea, whose entire population seemed to take to the streets whenever they played, creating a sea of red as the team dramatically beat Italy and Spain in the knockout stages. They eventually went down to Germany in the semi-finals, while Brazil ended England's challenge despite Michael Owen's early goal as Ronaldinho highlighted his precocious talent by chipping David Seaman from 25 yards. It was a disappointing end for Sven-Goran Eriksson's side as they went out with a whimper after a promising start. The Brazilians then brought Turkey's brave effort to an end to set up mouth-watering Final featuring the two most experienced World Cup nations. Amazingly, it was the first-ever meeting between Brazil and Germany in the tournament proper and provided the perfect opportunity for Ronaldo to erase the memories of his own personal nightmare in the 1998 Final in France. The script was already written and the star striker played his part by scoring both goals as the South Americans maintained their record of winning the trophy on every continent it has been played with a 2-0 win.

DATE	LOCATION	TEAMS	FULL/(HALF) TIME SCORE	VENUE
SEMI-FINALS				
26-JUN-02	SAITAMA	Brazil:Turkey	1:0 (0:0)	Saitama Stadium
25-JUN-02	SEOUL	Germany:Korea Republic	1:0 (0:0)	Seoul Stadium
MATCH FOR 3RD PLACE				
29-JUN-02	DAEGU	Korea Republic:Turkey	2:3 (1:3)	Daegu Stadium
FINAL				
30-JUN-02	YOKOHAMA	Germany:Brazil	0:2 (0:0)	International Stadium Yokohama

FAR LEFT: *Ronaldo - Brazil takes free kick*

TOP: *Ronaldo - Brazil scores his 1st goal against Germany. He would go on to score a second – his eighth of the tournament.*

ABOVE: *Ronaldinho - Brazil celebrates after winning the World Cup after victory over Germany*

RIGHT: *Cafu - Brazil celebrates after winning the World Cup after victory over Germany.*

BELOW: *Brazilian fans celebrate.*

ANGOLA

THE WEST Africans will be playing in their first ever World Cup Finals, but go into the tournament full of confidence after knocking Nigeria out in qualifying. The seeds of the surprise were sown way back in June 2004 when Nigeria were beaten 1-0 in Luanda. The Super Eagles had been strong favourites to progress, but Angola grew in confidence from that moment and held their nerve with a narrow final day win over Rwanda to seal their place in the showpiece event. The goalscorer in that famous triumph over Nigeria was skipper Fabrice 'Akwa' Maieco, who netted four more times in the group, and Angola will no doubt rely on him again in Germany.

Midfielder Gilberto is also a key figure and he proved his ability by helping Egyptian side Al Ahly reach the World Club Championships last December. However, the real secret to Angola's success was an amazing team-spirit and a strong work ethic instilled by coach Luis Oliveira Goncalves.

And although the Palancas Negros – or Black Antelopes - will be massive underdogs at the World Cup, just being there is a cause for celebration after 27 years of civil war that only came to an end in 2002.

ANGOLA

FOUNDED	1979
AFFILIATED	1980
WC PARTICIPATIONS	None
WC RECORD	No previous finals
CONTINENTAL TITLES	COSAFA Cup (1999 and 2001)
FIFA WORLD RANKING	62
COACH	Luis de Oliveir Goncalves
ROUTE TO GERMANY	Winners African Group Four
BOOKMAKERS ODDS	400-1

PLAYERS TO WATCH

TOP LEFT: *Fabrice Maceio Akwa Angola's deadly striker and captain with 30 goals for his country.*

TOP RIGHT: *Antonio Mendonca, a winger playing for Varzim in Portugal.*

LEFT: *Gilberto, a midfielder who plays for Al Ahli, in Egypt.*

ARGENTINA

ARGENTINA WILL be one of the favourites to lift the trophy on July 9, although it is 20 years since the South Americans last won the title. They were the first team to qualify from their continental group and eventually finished level with Brazil on an impressive 34 points from 18 games. The key to their progress was the goalscoring of Chelsea striker Hernan Crespo who netted seven times in qualifying, including a famous double against Brazil that sealed a place in Germany.

While Crespo grabbed many of the headlines, many pundits believe Juan Riquelme is the man who makes the team tick thanks to his superb vision and outstanding passing ability from an attacking midfield position. In spite of all that, a 3-2 friendly defeat to England last November and the 4-1 thrashing against Brazil in the 2005 Confederations Cup Final highlighted a few defensive frailties and manager Jose Pekerman will be hoping full-back Gabriel Heinze is fully fit for the World Cup matches. The Manchester United man was sidelined for months with a serious knee injury in the build-up to the tournament, but would be a major addition to the backline if he can recover in time.

ARGENTINA

FOUNDED	1893
AFFILIATED	1912
WC PARTICIPATIONS	13 (1930, 1934, 1958, 1962, 1966, 1974, 1978, 1982, 1986, 1990, 1994, 1998, 2002)
WC RECORD	Winners 1978, 1986, runners-up 1930, 1990
CONTINENTAL TITLES	Copa America 14 times (1921, 1925, 1927, 1927, 1937, 1941, 1945, 1946, 1947, 1955, 1957, 1959, 1991, 1993), Pan American Cup 6 times (1951, 1955, 1959, 1971, 1995, 2003)
FIFA WORLD RANKING	4
COACH	Jose Peckerman
ROUTE TO GERMANY	2nd South American Zone
BOOKMAKERS ODDS	13-2

PLAYERS TO WATCH

TOP LEFT: *Hernan Crespo. Argentina's top scorer in the qualifying matches with 7 Goals, Plays in the Premiership for Chelsea FC.*

TOP RIGHT: *Juan Roman Riquelme, Spanish Club Villerreal's brilliant midfielder.*

LEFT: *Argentina's Lionel Messi (R) challenges Qatar's Ali Nasser for the ball during their friendly soccer match in Al-sadd stadium in Doha, Qatar November 16, 2005. Argentina won 3-0. He plays his club football for FC Barcelona.*

ABOVE: *Australian soccer team members (L-R REAR) Brett Emerton, Mark Schwarzer, Tony Vidmar, Tony Popovic, Scott Chipperfield, Mark Viduka (L-R FRONT) Vincent Grella, Lucas Neill, Tim Cahill, Jason Culina and Marco Bresciano pose before the second World Cup qualifying tie at Stadium Australia in Sydney November 16, 2005.*

AUSTRALIA

AUSTRALIA FINALLY put years of frustration behind them to win a dramatic play-off against Uruguay and seal their place in Germany. Four years after defeat to the same opponents denied them a place in the World Cup Finals – and 32 years after their last appearance at the tournament – the Socceroos are back in the big time. The team has been growing in stature for the past decade with numerous players, such as Harry Kewell, Tim Cahill, Mark Schwarzer and Lucas Neill, proving their ability in the English Premiership. However, in spite of dominating the Oceania region, their undoing has been the play-off system with successive defeats to Argentina, Iran and Uruguay denying them a place in the last three World Cups. However, this time around they made it through against the South Americans, although they needed a penalty shoot-out following a nail-biting 1-1 draw over two legs.

Although the current players obviously lack experience on such a big stage, the Australia manager is no stranger to international success. Guus Hiddink, who remains head coach at PSV Eindhoven, became a national hero in South Korea when he led them to the World Cup semi-finals four years ago, a feat he had already achieved with Holland in 1998.

AUSTRALIA

FOUNDED	1961
AFFILIATED	1963
WC PARTICIPATIONS	1 (1974)
WC RECORD	Group Stage 1974
CONTINENTAL TITLES	Oceania Champions on three occasions (1980, 1996, 2000)
FIFA WORLD RANKING	49
COACH	Guus Hiddink (Holland)
ROUTE TO GERMANY	Winners South American Oceanian Play-offs
BOOKMAKERS ODDS	300-1

PLAYERS TO WATCH

TOP LEFT: *Tim Cahill. Oceania Player of the Year, the midfielder plays for Everton in the English Premiership.*

TOP RIGHT: *Mark Viduka. Striker of Croatian descent who plays for Middlesborough in England.*

LEFT: *Brett Emerton, Blackburn rovers wide midfielder.*

BRAZIL

THE HOLDERS will again be the team to beat in Germany – and anybody who can find a way to stop the breathtaking Brazilians will deserve the trophy. The attack-minded team averaged nearly two goals per game in qualifying and have an enviable array of talent going forward. Ronaldo's record speaks for itself, Adriano proved his undoubted ability in last summer's Confederations Cup, while youngster Robinho is ready to truly announce himself of the world stage.

As if that was not enough, defenders have to deal with the mesmerising trickery of Ronaldinho and the sublime vision of Kaka in midfield. Brazil were often accused in the past of being vulnerable at the back, but in Arsenal midfielder Gilberto they have found a solid shield, while Roque Junior is a no-nonsense centre-back capable of dealing with the roughest of centre-forwards. No surprise, therefore, that the bookmakers have long made the five-times champions hot favourites to claim the title again.

However, one glimmer of hope for all the other contenders is that Europe is not a happy hunting ground for the Brazilians, with only one triumph – way back in 1958 in Sweden - from nine attempts on the continent.

BRAZIL

FOUNDED	1914
AFFILIATED	1923
WC PARTICIPATIONS	17 (1930, 1934, 1938, 1950, 1954, 1958, 1962, 1966, 1970, 1974, 1978, 1982, 1986, 1990, 1994, 1998, 2002)
WC RECORD	Winners 1958, 1962, 1970, 1994, 2002, runners-up 1950, 1998
CONTINENTAL TITLES	Copa America 7 times (1919, 1922, 1949, 1989, 1993, 1997, 1999), Pan American Cup 4 times (1963, 1975 with Mexico, 1979, 1987)
FIFA WORLD RANKING	1
COACH	Carlos Alberto Parreira
ROUTE TO GERMANY	1st South American Zone
BOOKMAKERS ODDS	11-4 fav

PLAYERS TO WATCH

TOP LEFT: *Ronaldinho. Ronaldo de Assis Moreira (Little Ronaldo), European Footballer of the Year, Barcelona's brilliant playmaker.*

TOP RIGHT: *Adriano. Adriano Leite Ribeiro, Internazionale Striker.*

LEFT: *Kaka. Ricardo Izecson dos Santos Leite, A.C. Milan's attacking midfielder.*

COSTA RICA

COSTA RICA may be underdogs, but they have plenty of World Cup experience in their squad. The Central Americans are taking a very similar set of players to Germany as the group that went to the Far East in 2002. They may have gone out in the group stage four years ago, but they earned a draw against eventual semi-finalists Turkey and only missed out on a place in the knock-out rounds on goal difference.

Former West Ham and Manchester City striker Paulo Wanchope was one of the stars of that campaign and he is back again having since claimed the honour as Costa Rica's all-time record goalscorer. Stocky Ronald Gomez may not look like a prolific striker, but his sublime skill from free-kicks has brought stacks of goals and more than 100 caps in the process – an amazing feat also reached by defender Luis Marin. Midfielder Walter Centeno is another player with plenty of knowledge, having made his debut back in 1995, and he helped Deportivo Saprissa to the World Club Championships in Japan back in December.

The Costa Ricans will be led by manager Alexandre Guimaraes who was a member of the international side that reached the last 16 of the 1990 World Cup.

COSTA RICA

FOUNDED	1921
AFFILIATED	1921
WC PARTICIPATIONS	2 (1990, 2002)
WC RECORD	Best Second Round 1990
CONTINENTAL TITLES	Seven times CCCF champions (1941, 1946, 1948, 1953, 1955, 1960, 1961), three times Concacaf champions (1963, 1969, 1989), Central American champions (1993)
FIFA WORLD RANKING	21
COACH	Alexander Guimaraes
ROUTE TO GERMANY	3rd in CONCACAF Final Group
BOOKMAKERS ODDS	500-1

PLAYERS TO WATCH

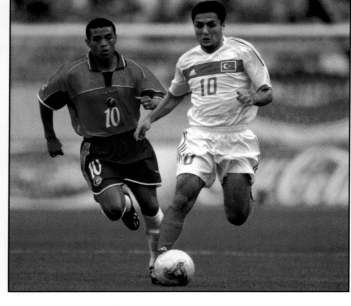

TOP LEFT: *Paulo Wanchope, who currently plays for Al-Garafah, in Qatar, the strikers previous clubs have included Derby, West Ham, Manchester City and Malaga.*

TOP RIGHT: *Walter Centeno (left), midfielder, who currently plays for Deportivo Saprissa.*

LEFT: *Rolando Fonseca Jiménez (left) striker for CSD Comunicaciones of the Guatemalan first division.*

CROATIA

CROATIA MAY struggle to equal or better their third-placed finish from 1998, but they could be dangerous opponents for one of the big guns in the group stages. The former Yugoslavian republic have suffered some major disappointments since that glorious tournament in France, but bounced back with an impressive qualification campaign. They were unbeaten and finished top of a group that contained Sweden, Bulgaria and Hungary. Coach Zlatko Kranjcar has galvanised the team into a strong unit, but will also be a proud father with son Niko one of the key members of the squad. The main goal threat is likely to come from Glasgow Rangers striker Dado Prso and former Aston Villa frontman Bosko Balaban.

Balaban was something of a flop in the Premiership, but has since resurrected his career at Bruges, while Prso averages a goal every other game in Scotland. At the back, Igor Tudor may well have left Italian giants Juventus for lesser lights Siena on loan, but he will be just 28-years-old going into the tournament and is still one of the most fearsome defenders in Europe. And however well Croatia do, their famous red and white check will provide a colourful addition to the World Cup party.

CROATIA

FOUNDED	1912
AFFILIATED	1992
WC PARTICIPATIONS	2 (1998, 2002)
WC RECORD	Semi-finals 1998
CONTINENTAL TITLES	None
FIFA WORLD RANKING	20
COACH	Zlatko Kranjcar
ROUTE TO GERMANY	Winners European Group 8
BOOKMAKERS ODDS	50-1

PLAYERS TO WATCH

TOP LEFT: *Igor Tudor, the Juventus defender.*

TOP RIGHT: *Bosko Balaban, signed for FC Bruges on a free transfer. In the 2004-2005 season he scored for them 11 times in 24 appearances.*

LEFT: *Dado Prso, a striker who plays his club football for FC Rangers in Scotland, having joined them on a free transfer from Monaco in the summer of 2004.*

CZECH REPUBLIC

THE CZECH republic are making their debut in the World Cup this year, but unlike some of the other newcomers they can expect to go a long way. Since splitting from Slovakia in 1993, the Czechs have attempted to qualify for the past two tournaments, but this will be their first appearance on the big stage. However, they have proved in the European Championships that they are a match for anyone - also highlighted by their dramatic rise to second in the official FIFA World Rankings.

In Pavel Nedved, Karel Poborsky and Vladimir Smicer, the Czechs have players with the experience of coming up against the best opponents on a regular basis and they will not fear anybody. But in addition the team is brimming with young talent such as striker Milan Baros, midfielder Tomas Rosicky and goalkeeper Petr Cech who have also proved themselves with big European club teams. It is true that they only qualified for the World Cup via a play-off victory over Norway, but that was largely down to being paired with a rejuvenated Holland team in the qualifiers who were unbeaten.

Make no mistake, the unseeded Czechs will be a team that every one of the so-called Big Boys will want to avoid and with a bit of luck and a favourable draw they could just find themselves still involved when the tournament heads into July.

CZECH REPUBLIC

FOUNDED	1901
AFFILIATED	1907
WC PARTICIPATIONS	8 (1934, 1938, 1954, 1958, 1962, 1970, 1982, 1990 as Czechoslovakia)
WC RECORD	Runners Up, 1934, 1962
CONTINENTAL TITLES	European champions (1976 as Czechoslovakia)
FIFA WORLD RANKING	2
COACH	Karel Bruckner
ROUTE TO GERMANY	European Play Off Winners
BOOKMAKERS ODDS	20-1

PLAYERS TO WATCH

TOP LEFT: *Pavel Nedved, European footballer of the year 2003 his Juventus' brilliant playmaker.*

TOP RIGHT: *Milan Baros, Aston Villa's striker won the golden boot in the 2004 European Championships with five goals.*

LEFT: *Petr Cech, Chelsea FC's brilliant goal keeper who has kept 21 clean sheets in only 37 appearances.*

ECUADOR

IF ECUADOR could have the World Cup Finals played in their home stadium in Quito they might be favourites to win. The South Americans have an amazing record at their own Estadio Olimpico Atahualpa, taking full advantage of their experience of playing in the depleted oxygen at 9,350 feet above sea level. Indeed, they were unbeaten in eight home qualifiers and won six of them, including victories over continental superpowers Brazil and Argentina. However, on the road it was a totally different story with just one win against Bolivia in La Paz – the highest capital in the world!

Germany is unlikely to provide the kind of environment that Ecuador thrive in, but coach Luis Suarez has assembled an experienced squad that could cause one or two upsets. Agustin Delgado, who is a much better player than his nightmare spell at Southampton suggests, and Edison Mendez will carry the weight of expectation of finishing the qualifying campaign as joint scorers with five goals apiece. Ecuador's main aim would appear to go one step further than four years ago when they made their debut at the Finals – only to lose their first two games to Italy and Mexico which made the win over Croatia relatively meaningless.

ECUADOR

FOUNDED	1925
AFFILIATED	1926
WC PARTICIPATIONS	1 (2002)
WC RECORD	Group Stage 2002
CONTINENTAL TITLES	None
FIFA WORLD RANKING	37
COACH	Luis Fernando Suarez
ROUTE TO GERMANY	3rd South American Zone
BOOKMAKERS ODDS	125-1

PLAYERS TO WATCH

TOP LEFT: *Edison Mendez, midfielder who currently plays for Ecuadorian league club Liga Deportiva Universitaria (Quito).*

TOP RIGHT: *Ivan Kaviedes, Possibly Ecuador's most exciting young talent, the Guayaquil forward in the Ecuador league.*

LEFT: *Ulises De La Cruz, Aston Villa FC's enterprising midfielder.*

ENGLAND

EXPECTATIONS ARE again high that England can turn the clock back to 1966 and lift the World Cup trophy. A youthful, yet vastly experienced, squad has shown glimpses of being able to win the tournament in recent years – although there have also been some worryingly woeful performances as well.

Key to success for the Three Lions is likely to be Wayne Rooney who was just 16-years-old when Sven-Goran Eriksson's side lost to Brazil in the quarter-finals last time out.

The Manchester United striker is one of the most exciting talents in Europe and has struck up a great partnership with Michael Owen, a veteran in relative terms at the age of just 26. England's defence should be one of the strongest in Germany, with Sol Campbell, Rio Ferdinand and John Terry all rated as world-class and battling for just two centre-back positions, while Ashley Cole provides an attacking option from full-back. The biggest problem for Eriksson is likely to be formulating an effective plan that utilises all his excellent midfielders. Doubts remain as to whether Steven Gerrard and Frank Lampard can play together in the middle, skipper David Beckham increasingly prefers not to play wide on the right, while no-one has yet adequately filled the problem left side. However, it all adds up to the fact that England have possibly the best chance of winning the trophy since that famous day 40 years ago.

ENGLAND

FOUNDED	1863
AFFILIATED	1905
WC PARTICIPATIONS	11 (1950, 1954, 1958, 1962, 1966, 1970, 1982, 1986, 1990, 1998, 2002)
WC RECORD	Winners 1966
CONTINENTAL TITLES	None
FIFA WORLD RANKING	9
COACH	Sven Goran Ericsson (Sweden)
ROUTE TO GERMANY	Winners European Group 6
BOOKMAKERS ODDS	7-1

PLAYERS TO WATCH

TOP LEFT: *Wayne Rooney, Manchester United forward. He beat James Prinsep's 124-year record as England's youngest player when he made his debut against Australia on 12 February 2003 aged 17 years and 111 days. Seven months later, he became England's youngest ever scorer when – aged 17 years and 317 days – he struck the opening goal in a UEFA European Championship qualifying win away to FYR Macedonia.*

TOP RIGHT: *Frank Lampard, Chelsea FC midfielder. Englands highest scorer with five goals in the qualifying stages. Jose Mourinho, manager of Chelsea FC believes that his midfielder is the best player in the world.*

LEFT: *John Terry, Chelsea FC defender. Chelsea's captain, the most solid central defender in the world and undoutably a future England captain.*

FRANCE

THE 1998 champions will want to put a nightmare four years behind them and prove they are still one of the best teams in the world. Heading into the 2002 tournament in the Far East, things couldn't have been much better for the holders but their shocking performances in South Korea sparked a dramatic slump.

France also surrendered their European Championship title with a whimper in 2004 and head to Germany on the back of a shaky qualification campaign that included draws against Israel and Switzerland.

Indeed, such was their plight that they looked set to miss out on a place in Germany, before midfield maestro Zinedine Zidane came out of retirement and eased the nerves.

However, with the likes of Thierry Henry, Patrick Vieira, Lilian Thuram, William Gallas, David Trezeguet and Djibril Cisse at their disposal, it would be foolish to suggest the French are not still one of the favourites this time around.

And many of Les Blues supporters highlight the fact their form was poor going into the 1998 World Cup Finals, only for the side to gain strength as the tournament progressed before that famous victory over Brazil sparked wild scenes across the country.

FRANCE

FOUNDED	1919
AFFILIATED	1904
WC PARTICIPATIONS	11 (1930, 1934, 1938, 1954, 1958, 1966, 1978, 1982, 1986, 1998, 2002)
WC RECORD	Winners 1998
CONTINENTAL TITLES	2 times European champions (1984, 2000)
FIFA WORLD RANKING	5
COACH	Raymond Domenech
ROUTE TO GERMANY	Winners European Group 4
BOOKMAKERS ODDS	12-1

PLAYERS TO WATCH

TOP LEFT: *Thierry Henry. The Arsenal forward is considered one of the most dynamic attacking players in the game today and should Arsenal ever decide to let him go he could become the most expensive player in world history.*

TOP RIGHT: *David Trezeguet, Frances excellent striker who plays for Juventus, with whom he won the Serie A title three times.*

LEFT: *Patrick Vieira was finally tempted away from Highbury. Arsenal accepted a bid of €20m (£13.7m) from Italian giants Juventus on July 14, 2005, and Vieira agreed a five-year contract with the Serie A side the following day.*
With Vieira, Juventus coach Fabio Capello hopes to improve his midfield together with the Brazilian Emerson and Czech Pavel Nedved.

GERMANY

HOSTING THE tournament may give Germany an extra edge, while their previous World Cup record speaks for itself. However, it is clear that the three-time champions are still in a transition period as they attempt to build a team to truly rival their legendary line-ups. Veterans such as Oliver Kahn and Oliver Neuville remain and in Michael Ballack they have one of the best midfielders on the planet, but many of the other squad members are inexperienced and untested.

Youngsters such as energetic ball-winner Bastian Schweinsteiger and powerful defender Robert Huth have shown some excellent promise, but even the German Football Association have acknowledged that simply reaching the quarter-finals would be a good achievement. However, with former star striker Juergen Klinsmann at the helm, the hosts will not go down without a fight and they may well highlight the fact they were rank underdogs heading into the last World Cup. In spite of some the same kind of criticisms in the Far East, the Germans picked a path all the way to the Final where they were only beaten by the outstanding Brazil outfit. Therefore, the doubters may well write off Germany again at their peril this time around.

GERMANY

FOUNDED	1900
AFFILIATED	1904
WC PARTICIPATIONS	15 (1934, 1938, 1954, 1958, 1962, 1966, 1970, 1974, 1978, 1982, 1986, 1990, 1994, 1998, 2002)
WC RECORD	Winner 1954, 1974, 1990
CONTINENTAL TITLES	Three times European champions (1972, 1980, 1996)
FIFA WORLD RANKING	16
COACH	Jurgen Klinsman
ROUTE TO GERMANY	Host Nation
BOOKMAKERS ODDS	8-1

PLAYERS TO WATCH

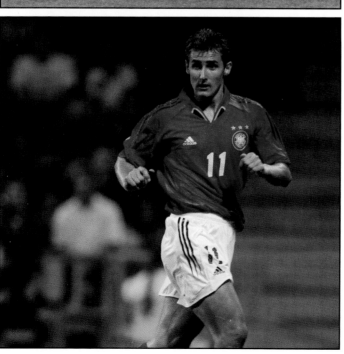

TOP LEFT: *Michael Ballack, Bayarn Munich's influential midfielder who is rumoured to be joining Man Utd. in the summer.*

TOP RIGHT: *Oliver Kahn, Bayern Munich's goalkeeper has been capped for his country 56 times.*

LEFT: *Miroslav Klose, top scoring stirker playing for Werder Bremen in the Bundes Liga.*

GHANA

MICHAEL ESSIEN may be the most famous Ghanaian heading into the 2006 World Cup, but expect a few of his team-mates to grab a few headlines of their own when the tournament kicks-off. Essien will attract the spotlight after last summer's high profile £24.4m move to Chelsea and he will no doubt drive the midfield, but there are plenty of other dangermen ready to pounce.

Defender Sammy Kuffour is a Champions League winner with Bayern Munich, while Abubakari Yakubu and Anthony Obodai have both been impressive for Ajax.

Striker Isaac Boakye has also caught the eye in the German Bundesliga despite playing for unfashionable Armenia Bielefeld, while partner Asamoah Gyan has done the same thing in Italy with Modena.

In midfield, meanwhile, Essien can expect strong assistance from Stephen Appiah who had two decent seasons with Juventus before switching to Fenerbahce. All that means Ratomir Dujkovic's Black Cats will pose a strong threat to some of the major nations this summer. Perhaps the biggest surprise is not Ghana's appearance in Germany, but the fact it has taken them so long to reach their first World Cup given the fact they have won the African Nations Cup no fewer than four times.

GHANA

FOUNDED	1957
AFFILIATED	1958
WC PARTICIPATIONS	None
WC RECORD	No previous Finals
CONTINENTAL TITLES	African Cup of Nations (1963, 1965, 1978, 1982), CSSA Nations Cup (1982-1984, 1986, 1987)
FIFA WORLD RANKING	50
COACH	Ratomir Dujkovic (Serbia & Montenegro)
ROUTE TO GERMANY	Winners African Group 2
BOOKMAKERS ODDS	200-1

PLAYERS TO WATCH

TOP LEFT: *Samuel Kuffour, strong central defender, who is Bayern Munich's longest serving player alongside Mehmet Scholl. Kuffour was named Ghanain player of the year in '98, and '99.*

TOP RIGHT: *Michael Essien,the most versatile midfielder in the premiership was Chelsea FC's record signing from Lyon in the summer.*

LEFT: *Stephen Appiah, combative midfielder In the summer he left Juventus for Turkish champions Fenerbahçe SK in an €8m transfer.*

HOLLAND

THE DUTCH look back to their brilliant best as they attempt to erase the horror of not even qualifying for the World Cup four years ago. That failure seems to have sparked a fire under Holland, though, and they made it to Germany with the best record of any European team - an amazing 32 points from 12 games with just three goals conceded.

Manchester United striker Ruud van Nistelrooy unsurprisingly led the goalscoring with seven, but all the Dutch players seem to have raised their game to counter the criticism that had come their way. Under coach Marco van Basten, they look especially strong in midfield with captain Phillip Cocu providing the anchor, while Rafael van der Vaart and winger Arjen Robben cause countless problems going forward. Such has been the competition for places that talents such as Edgar Davids and Marc van Bommel have been regularly left out of the team. The defence has been re-built with Ajax duo John Heitinga and Nigel De Jong ably assisted by Khalid Bouhlarouz who has made massive strides forward since moving from Waalwijk to Hamburg in 2004.

Behind them is the veteran goalkeeper Edwin van der Sar who has also had a renewed lease of life after joining Manchester United last summer.

HOLLAND

FOUNDED	1889
AFFILIATED	1904
WC PARTICIPATIONS	7 (1934, 1938, 1974, 1978, 1990, 1994, 1998)
WC RECORD	Runners Up 1974, 1978
CONTINENTAL TITLES	European champions (1988)
FIFA WORLD RANKING	3
COACH	Marco van Basten
ROUTE TO GERMANY	Winners European Group 1
BOOKMAKERS ODDS	11-1

PLAYERS TO WATCH

TOP LEFT: *Ruud van Nistelrooy, (full name Rutgerus Johannes Martinus van Nistelrooij) Man Utd. Wiley striker, he tends to score all of his goals from inside of the twenty yard box having scored only once in the premiership from outside of the box.*

TOP RIGHT: *Arjen Robben, Chelsea FC's majestic winger.*

LEFT: *Mark Van Bommel, FC Barcelona's influential midfielder.*

IRAN

MEHDI MAHDAVIKIA and Vahid Hashemian could provide Iran with some inside knowledge in Germany this summer. The pair both ply their trade for top clubs in the Bundesliga - Hashemian for Bayern Munich and Mahdavikia with Hamburg - and will be key to Iran's hopes of qualifying for the knock-out stages.

Two more Iranians, Ali Karimi and Ferydoon Zandi also play in Germany, so the team has plenty of experience in the stadiums that will host this year's tournament. Iran will also boast the highest goalscorer in the history of international football - striker Ali Daei who has more than 100 for Team Melli. That puts him well above the likes of legends such as Ferenc Puskas (84), Pele (77) and Gerd Muller (68) and, at the age of 37, he will want to go out on a high in this World Cup.

All those players were instrumental in helping the side book their place in Germany with a game to spare, finishing narrowly behind Japan in their section. Iran, who featured in this tournament in 1978 and 1998, are unlikely to be overawed, but Croatian coach Branko Ivankovic will have to get his hard-working team playing at their very best if they want to make it through the group stages for the first time in their history.

IRAN

FOUNDED	1920
AFFILIATED	1945
WC PARTICIPATIONS	2 (1978, 1998)
WC RECORD	Group Stage 1978, 1998
CONTINENTAL TITLES	Asian Championships 3 times (1968, 1972, 1976), Asian Games 4 times (1974, 1990, 1998, 2002)
FIFA WORLD RANKING	19
COACH	Branko Ivankovic (Croatia)
ROUTE TO GERMANY	Runners Up Asian Group B
BOOKMAKERS ODDS	500-1

PLAYERS TO WATCH

TOP LEFT: *Ali Daei has joined the exclusive circle of players with a Century of Caps. In a November 28, 2003 Asian Cup qualifier in Tehran against Lebanon, he scored his 85th international goal he plays for Saba Battery in Tehran.*

TOP RIGHT: *Mehdi Mahdavikia, the right winger currently plays for SV Hamburg in Germany, having been signed for that club in 2000.*

LEFT: *Vahid Hashemian ("The Helicopter") currently plays for Hannover of the German Bundesliga.*

ITALY

NO WORLD cup would be complete without the passion and drama of Italy. The three-time champions never fail to fascinate, for their sublime skills but also for the turmoil and controversy that often accompanies their games. Watching the Italians is never dull. Most recent examples include the surprise defeat to South Korea four years ago and the penalty shoot-out heartbreak against France in the 1998 quarter-finals.

But with three titles from the nine tournaments held in Europe, and with the Finals now in Germany, Italy will fancy their chances of grabbing the headlines for all the right reasons.

They certainly have an enviable squad to choose from. Goals should not be a problem with the likes of Francesco Totti, Christian Vieri and rising stars Alberto Gilardino and Luca Toni vying for places.

There is plenty of creativity in midfield thanks to Genarro Gattuso, Gianluca Zambrotta and Andrea Pirlo, but it is at the back where Italy will aim to truly conquer their rivals.

In Alessandro Nesta and Fabio Cannavaro they have two of the best centre-backs in the world and coach Marcello Lippi - not to mention a demanding Italian public - will expect them to again be the rock on which the Azzurri challenge is built.

ITALY

FOUNDED	1898
AFFILIATED	1905
WC PARTICIPATIONS	15 (1934, 1938, 1950, 1954, 1962, 1966, 1970, 1974, 1978, 1982, 1986, 1990, 1994, 1998, 2002)
WC RECORD	Winners 1934, 1938, 1982
CONTINENTAL TITLES	European champions (1968)
FIFA WORLD RANKING	12
COACH	Marcello Lippi
ROUTE TO GERMANY	Winners European Group 5
BOOKMAKERS ODDS	9-1

PLAYERS TO WATCH

TOP LEFT: *Alessandro Del Piero, the Juventus captain has been on fine form for his country scoring 24 goals in 67 appearances.*

TOP RIGHT: *Francesco Totti, the AS Roma player is an attacking midfielder but also deadly from free kicks.*

LEFT: *Alessandro Nesta, the AC Milan center back has amazing tackling skill, game reading ability and is widely considered one of the best defenders in the world.*

IVORY COAST

DIDIER DROGBA and Kolo Toure have propelled the Ivory Coast into the consciousness of anyone who follows the English Premiership - and now their nation is hoping to make an impact on the world stage. Under the Chelsea striker and Arsenal defender, the west Africans have been improving rapidly and that was highlighted in qualifying when they topped a group that included five-time World Cup participants Cameroon. And they proved they will be no push-over against well organised European nations in Germany when they quickly followed that up with a 1-1 draw against Italy in a friendly back in November. Drogba scored in that game and will be the main goal threat, although strike partner Aruna Dindane netted seven times in qualifying and is also a major danger.

Kolo Toure is the key to the defence, although he is ably assisted by Arsenal team-mate Emmaneul Eboue, while brother Yaya also has a good chance of being involved as well. Perhaps the most vital player, though, is Bonaventure Kalou who links the defence and attack in his advanced midfield role and coach Henri Michel - who has previously managed France, Morocco and Cameroon at the World Cup - will be hoping he is on form if they are to spring a few surprises.

IVORY COAST

FOUNDED	1960
AFFILIATED	1960
WC PARTICIPATIONS	None
WC RECORD	No previous finals
CONTINENTAL TITLES	Cup of Nations (1992)
FIFA WORLD RANKING	41
COACH	Henri Michel
ROUTE TO GERMANY	Winners African Group 3
BOOKMAKERS ODDS	66-1

PLAYERS TO WATCH

TOP LEFT: *Didier Drogba, the Chelsea striker is considered one of the most powerful forwards around. He will cause undoubted problems for many a defender.*

TOP RIGHT: *Kolo Toure, the defender is regarded as the second fastest player at Arsenal, slower only than Thierry Henry.*

LEFT: *Bonaventure Kalou, Paris Saint-Germain's highly exciting attacking midfielder.*

JAPAN

JAPAN HAVE plenty to live up to after a successful run on home soil four years ago. Victories over Russia and Tunisia saw them through to the knock-out stage where they were only beaten 1-0 by eventual semi-finalists Turkey. Since then, they have won the 2004 Asian Cup and performed superbly at the 2005 Confederations Cup where they beat Greece and held mighty Brazil to a 2-2 draw. However, the qualifying campaign for Germany was far from convincing and they will need to find some more goals if they want to at least repeat the achievements of 2002.

Shunsuke Nakamura is the new play-making star, while Alessandro Santos - or Alex - is a naturalised Brazilian whose versatility means he can play in virtually any position. Shinji Ono could also be one to watch, having broken through four years ago, but he has suffered injury problems in the build up to this tournament. Veteran Hidetoshi Nakata also has something to prove after an unspectacular start to his career at Bolton.

One criticism previously levelled at the Japanese was that for all their undoubted possessed in skill, they lacked physical presence. However Junichi Inamoto, Yasuhito Endo and Tsuneyasu Miyamoto are three players not afraid to get stuck in and win the ball back for their creative team-mates.

JAPAN

FOUNDED	1921
AFFILIATED	1929
WC PARTICIPATIONS	2 (1998, 2002)
WC RECORD	2nd Round 2002
CONTINENTAL TITLES	Asian Cup twice (1992, 2000)
FIFA WORLD RANKING	15
COACH	Zico (Brazil)
ROUTE TO GERMANY	Winners Asian Group B
BOOKMAKERS ODDS	125-1

PLAYERS TO WATCH

TOP LEFT: *Junichi Inamoto, midfielder ex Arsenal and Fulham player, now with West Bromwich Albion.*

TOP RIGHT: *Yoshi Kawaguchi, the Japanese goalkeeper plays for Nordsjælland of the Danish league.*

LEFT: *Hidetoshi Nakata. Nakata has moved to England in August 2005 to try his luck in the Premiership with a loan spell at Bolton Wanderers.*

MEXICO

COACH RICARDO Lavolpe had promised that Mexico would qualify for the 2006 World Cup at a canter and it was a pledge that proved easy to fulfil. El Tricolor – as the national team is known – cruised to Germany as they finished six points clear of third-placed Costa Rica in the final CONCACAF group. That came after six straight wins, with just one goal conceded, in the previous stage.

Goals did not prove any problem at all, with three Mexico players in the top five of the CONCACAF scoring charts. Jared Borgetti, the Bolton striker, finished top with 14, while Jaime Lozano and Jose Fonseca hit 11 and 10 respectively. Although the opposition is likely to be stronger at the World Cup, defenders will have to be on their guard against those three attack-minded players, with Sergio Santana also a decent finisher from his deeper role.

To highlight their progress, the central Americans performed superbly at the 2005 Confederations Cup where they beat mighty Brazil in the group stages and held Argentina to a 1-1 draw in the semi-finals before slipping out on penalties.

All that augurs well and highlights could include defender Rafael Márquez and midfielder Hugo Sanchez – although he is sadly not renowned for somersaulting like his famous namesake who was a legend of Mexican football.

MEXICO

FOUNDED	1927
AFFILIATED	1929
WC PARTICIPATIONS	12 (1930, 1950, 1954, 1958, 1962, 1966, 1970, 1978, 1986, 1994, 1998, 2002)
WC RECORD	Quarter-finals 1970, 1986
CONTINENTAL TITLES	Three times NAFC champions (1947, 1949, 1991), three times CONCACAF champions (1965, 1971, 1977), three times Gold Cup (1993, 1996, 1998), five times Central American champions (1935, 1938, 1959, 1966, 1990), three times Pan American champions (1967, 1975 with Brazil, 1999)
FIFA WORLD RANKING	7
COACH	Ricardo Lavolpe (Argentina)
ROUTE TO GERMANY	Second CONCACAF Final Group
BOOKMAKERS ODDS	50-1

PLAYERS TO WATCH

TOP LEFT: *Jared Borgetti, striker currently playing for Bolton Wanderers F.C., whom he joined in the summer of 2005 for £900,000.*

TOP RIGHT: *Francisco Fonseca, a Striker from Club Cruz Azul in Mexico, is the hottest property in Mexican football and is the country's most popular player since the diminutive shot-stopper Jorge Campos.*

LEFT: *Hugo Sánchez Guerrero plays for UANL Tigres.*

PARAGUAY

THE SECOND round has been the stumbling block for Paraguay in the past two World Cups – and they will have to be on top form to go further this time. Four years ago the South Americans were beaten 1-0 by Germany and in 1998 they suffered a similar defeat to hosts France. Both of those opponents went on to reach the Final, so teams may well be pleased to face Paraguay if they make it through the group stage.

The Guarani's main man is likely to be striker Roque Santa Cruz who will want to do well in Germany given the fact he plays for Bayern Munich. He scored four goals in qualifying, but suffered a knee injury in October and question-marks will remain over his fitness.

If Santa Cruz is not on top form, the burden will be carried by strike partner Jose Cardoza who was impressive during the qualifying games. However, he will be 35 by the time the World Cup kicks-off so youngster Nelson Haedo Valdez may be given the chance to make his big breakthrough. Other key players are likely to be midfielder Diego Gavilan, who is better than his ill-fated spell at Newcastle suggested, and powerful defender Julio Cesar Caceres.

PARAGUAY

FOUNDED	1906
AFFILIATED	1921
WC PARTICIPATIONS	6 (1930, 1950, 1958, 1986, 1998, 2002)
WC RECORD	2nd Round 1998, 2002
CONTINENTAL TITLES	Copa America twice (1953, 1979)
FIFA WORLD RANKING	30
COACH	Anibal Ruiz (Uraguay)
ROUTE TO GERMANY	4th South American Zone
BOOKMAKERS ODDS	125-1

PLAYERS TO WATCH

TOP LEFT: *Roque Santa Cruz, is a striker, who currently plays for Bayern Munich of the German Bundesliga. He started playing for the Paraguayan national team at only 17.*

TOP RIGHT: *Diego Gavilan, former Newcastle and Udinese midfielder plays for his former club Brazilian Internacional Porto Alegre.*

LEFT: *Julio Cesar Caceres, established defender formerly played for FC Nantes in France before moving to Brazilian club Atletico Mineiro for the 2005/06 season.*

POLAND

POLAND HAVE twice finished third in the World Cup, but few expect them to repeat that achievement this time around. The highlights for the Poles came in 1974 and 1982, but since then they have hardly made an impact at the highest level and returned from the 2002 tournament with just a solitary victory over USA to their name. However, they showed in qualifying for Germany that under coach Pawel Janas they are enjoying something of a resurgence and they pushed much-fancied England all the way before booking their place as one of the best group runners-up. Key to that success was the seven goals apiece for Maciej Zurawski - who has made a great impact since joining Celtic - and Tomas Frankowski. They are ably assisted by Gregorz Rasiak whose performances helped earn him a move to Tottenham.

At the back, veteran captain Jacek Bak is the rock on which the defensive unit is still built, while Jerzy Dudek could prove vital if Poland are involved in a penalty shoot-out.

Coach Janas was one of the members of the 1982 Poland squad who claimed third place in the World Cup, but qualifying from the group stages will probably represent a decent return for the current side.

POLAND

FOUNDED	1919
AFFILIATED	1923
WC PARTICIPATIONS	6 (1938, 1974, 1978, 1982, 1986, 2002)
WC RECORD	3rd 1974, 1982
CONTINENTAL TITLES	None
FIFA WORLD RANKING	23
COACH	Pawel Janas
ROUTE TO GERMANY	Runners-up European Group 6
BOOKMAKERS ODDS	80-1

PLAYERS TO WATCH

TOP LEFT: *Jerzy Dudek, Liverpools hero goalkeeper with his performance in the Championship League final against AC Milan last year will be looking to continue the same vein of form in the World Cup.*

TOP RIGHT: *Jacek Bak, Polands veteran defender with spells at Olympique Lyonnais and RC Lens currently plays for Qatar club side Al-YYan.*

LEFT: *Gregorz Rasiak, Tottenham striker having moved from Derby County in the summer has been overshadowed by Mido and Keane at Spurs this season with be certainly fresh for the World Cup final.*

PORTUGAL

THE GOLDEN generation have largely gone, but Portugal have perhaps their best-ever chance of challenging for the World Cup. The Portuguese spent nearly a decade waiting for their 1991 World Youth Cup winning team to translate that success onto the big stage, but it never truly materialised and the likes of Rui Costa, Joao Pinto and Jorge Costa have now been replaced. However, with youngsters like Cristiano Ronaldo, Deco and Maniche the future looks bright and hopes have never been higher.

And they can still count on the mercurial Luis Figo, while the defence looks much stronger than in recent years with Chelsea duo Paulo Ferreira and Ricardo Carvalho flanking the no-nonsense centre-back Jorge Andrade. Expectations were raised even higher when Portugal qualified with ease, unbeaten in 12 games and top scorers in the European zone.

They also boasted the individual top scorer across the continental qualifiers, with Pauleta smashing 11 goals to highlight his own ability. Despite this being only Portugal's fourth-ever World Cup, they can take confidence from reaching the Final of Euro2004 on home soil – despite the eventual defeat to Greece – and it would be a massive shock if they did not go further than last time when they failed to reach the knock-out stages after losing to USA and South Korea.

PORTUGAL

FOUNDED	1914
AFFILIATED	1923
WC PARTICIPATIONS	3 (1966, 1986, 2002)
WC RECORD	3rd 1966
CONTINENTAL TITLES	None
FIFA WORLD RANKING	10
COACH	Luiz Felipe Scolari (Brazil)
ROUTE TO GERMANY	Winners European Group 3
BOOKMAKERS ODDS	20-1

PLAYERS TO WATCH

TOP LEFT: *Cristiano Ronaldo, Man Utd.'s exciting winger bought from Sporting Lisbon for £12.24 million.*

TOP RIGHT: *Nuno Gomes, (real name Nuno Miguel Soares Pereira Ribeiro) Benfica's prolific goal scorer. He uses the name Gomes after his childhood hero Fernando Gomes.*

LEFT: *Deco, (real name Anderson Luiz de Sousa) came to fame playing under Jose Mourinho at FC Porto but rather than follow his former coach to premiership side Chelsea he joined FC Barcelona instead.*

SAUDI ARABIA

SAUDI ARABIA will be playing in their fourth consecutive World Cup Finals, but they will want to avoid the kind of nightmare they suffered four years ago. The Sons of the Desert were thrashed 8-0 by Germany in their opening game and returned home three defeats and no goals to their name. However, they regrouped and qualified for this tournament in comfortable style, thanks largely to two impressive victories over the highly-rated South Koreans.

Their main strength in the Asian group was defence, with the likes of Redha Fallatha, Hamad Al Montashari, Naif Al Qadi and especially goalkeeper Mabrouk Zaid helping the side concede just two goals in 12 qualifying games.

They are all relative newcomers in a team that has been reshaped since the last World Cup, but legendary Sami Al Jaber remains a big part. The striker, who has more than 150 caps which made him the sixth most experienced footballer in international history at the end of 2005, is likely to feature despite heading into the tournament aged 33.

However, Mohammad Al Shloub and Ibrahim Al Shahrani have taken over as the main goalscorers in the team - claiming three apiece in the qualification matches.

Coach Gabriel Calderon, a former Argentine international, will hope they are on target in Germany to give the Saudis a chance to prove they are better than their most recent appearance in the Finals suggested.

SAUDI ARABIA

FOUNDED	1959
AFFILIATED	1959
WC PARTICIPATIONS	3 (1994, 1998, 2002)
WC RECORD	2nd Round 1994
CONTINENTAL TITLES	Asian Cup 3 times (1984, 1988, 1996), Gulf Cup twice (1994, 2002)
FIFA WORLD RANKING	32
COACH	Gabriel Calderon (Argentina)
ROUTE TO GERMANY	Winners Asian Group A
BOOKMAKERS ODDS	500-1

PLAYERS TO WATCH

TOP LEFT: *Sami Al Jaber, Saudi Arabian striker plays for Al-Hilal. He has played 152 international matches for Saudi Arabia and scored 42 goals for the national team and is its captain.*

TOP RIGHT: *Mohammad Al Shloub, the diminutive midfielder for Al-Hilal helped Saudi Arabia on their way to Germany with a comprehensive 3-0 victory over Uzbekistan before an impressive crowd of 75,000 at the King Fahd International stadium in Ryadh.*

LEFT: *Ahmed Al Bahri, Saudi Arabia's young defender plays for club side Al Basha.*

SERBIA & MONTENEGRO

SERBIA ARE celebrating their first ever World Cup, although they can trace a long and successful history in the tournament as the former Yugoslavia. The modern Serbian nation only came into existence in 2003, but boasts a string of top-class players in some of the biggest leagues across Europe.

Mateja Kezman may not have made a massive impact at Chelsea, but he grabbed five goals in qualifying as Serbia finished above Spain in their group to guarantee their place in Germany. Portsmouth's Zvonimir Vukic was not far behind with four, while the attacking options also include Savo Milosevic. However, qualifying results suggest that Serbia's main strength will be in defence after they conceded just one goal in 10 games. Players such as Mladen Krstajic, Nemanja Vidic and Goran Gavrancic may not be household names, but they have been in superb form in front of highly-rated goalkeeper Dragoslav Jevric.

Linking the play is midfield maestro Dejan Stankovic, although plenty of opponents in Serie A will agree that he is also not afraid to make strong tackles to win possession back before setting up attacks.

Leading the Plavi – or Blues - is coach Ilija Petkovic, a former Yugoslavian international himself, who admits he has told his squad to stop being artists and become workers instead and the plan appears to be working.

SERBIA & MONTENEGRO

FOUNDED	1919
AFFILIATED	1919
WC PARTICIPATIONS	7 (1930, 1950, 1958, 1962, 1974, 1990, 1998 as Yugoslavia)
WC RECORD	Semi-finals 1930
CONTINENTAL TITLES	None
FIFA WORLD RANKING	47
COACH	Illija Petkovic
ROUTE TO GERMANY	Winners European Group 7
BOOKMAKERS ODDS	66-1

PLAYERS TO WATCH

TOP LEFT: *Mateja Kezman, former Chelsea striker back to his best now playing for Athletico De Madrid.*

TOP RIGHT: *Savo Milosevic, Aston Villa's ex-striker now playing for Osasuna, a Spanish Primera División football.*

LEFT: *Dejan Stankovic, is a midfielder who currently plays for Inter Milan.*

SOUTH KOREA

DICK ADVOCAAT may struggle to repeat the World Cup heroics of Guus Hiddink four years ago, but South Korea will still be a force to be reckoned with. Hiddink was in charge as the Taeguk Warriors beat Portugal, Spain and Italy en route to an amazing appearance in the semi-final where they were only narrowly knocked out by Germany. Humberto Coelho found the task of replacing Hiddink too difficult and he was released midway through qualifying by Jo Bonfrere, who then surprisingly resigned once a place in Germany had been assured, with Advocaat then taking over.

The managerial merry-go-round is unlikely to disrupt a talented squad, with Park Ji-Sung's displays at international level and with PSV Eindhoven in the Champions League earning him deserved plaudits and a move to Manchester United.

Former PSV team-mate Lee Young-Pyo has also moved to the Premiership after being snapped up by Tottenham, while Lee Woon-Jae is widely rated as one of the best Asian goalkeepers.

Korea's superb run on home soil in 2002 was aided by a wave of support as fans turned the streets red whenever the team played. That may not be the case in Germany and it will be interesting to see what effect that has on results.

SOUTH KOREA

FOUNDED	1945
AFFILIATED	1948
WC PARTICIPATIONS	6 (1954, 1986, 1990, 1994, 1998, 2002)
WC RECORD	Semi-finals 2002
CONTINENTAL TITLES	Asian Cup twice (1956, 1960), Asian Games 3 times (1970 together with Burma, 1978 together with Korea DPR, 1986)
FIFA WORLD RANKING	29
COACH	Dick Advocat (Holland)
ROUTE TO GERMANY	Second Asian Group A
BOOKMAKERS ODDS	300-1

PLAYERS TO WATCH

TOP LEFT: *Park Ji-Sung, a summer buy for Man Utd., the ex PSV Eindhoven winger used to be a defensive midfielder until Guus Hiddink the South Korean coach moved him up the pitch.*

TOP RIGHT: *Lee Young-Pyo, Tottenham defender moved from PSV Eindhoven in the summer*

LEFT: *Lee Woon-Jae, currently playing for Suwon Samsung Bluewings in the Korean K-League as a goalkeeper. He has represented the Korean National football team since the 1992 Summer Olympics in Barcelona.*

SPAIN

COULD THIS be the year that Spain finally realise their undoubted potential on the world stage? It is predicted before every tournament and they must surely come good eventually. It is amazing that in a country that boasts one of the best leagues in Europe, with star-studded club sides such as Real Madrid and Barcelona, the national team have reached just one World Cup semi-final – and that way back in 1950.

However, the omens were not good in 2004 as Luis Aragone's side finished behind Serbia and Montenegro in their qualifying group and needed a play-off win over Slovakia to even book their place in Germany.

It was a frustrating campaign for a squad packed with talent, especially going forward, although perhaps part of the problem has been a failure to stick with a settled strike partnership. Raul, who suffered serious knee ligament damage in November, had been the number one choice, but Albert Luque, Jose Antonio Reyes, Fernando Morientes, David Villa and Fernando Torres were all used as well in some kind of combination.

At least the defence has been more stable with full-backs Asier del Horno and Michel Salgado flanking centre-backs Carlos Puyol and Carlos Marchena in front of athletic goalkeeper Iker Casillas. If all the pieces click into place Spain could finally be a force to be reckoned with and throw off the tag of one of the best teams never to win the World Cup.

SPAIN

FOUNDED	1913
AFFILIATED	1934
WC PARTICIPATIONS	11 (1934, 1950, 1962, 1966, 1978, 1982, 1986, 1990, 1994, 1998, 2002)
WC RECORD	4th Place 1950
CONTINENTAL TITLES	European champions
FIFA WORLD RANKING	6
COACH	Luis Aragones
ROUTE TO GERMANY	European Play Off Winners
BOOKMAKERS ODDS	16-1

PLAYERS TO WATCH

TOP LEFT: *Fernando Torres, he is nicknamed El Niño (The Child), because of his youth. The striker plays for Atlético de Madrid.*

TOP RIGHT: *Javier Luis Garcia, currently plays for Liverpool FC. His ability to kick confidently with both feet makes him an extremely versatile attacker, deployable on both flanks, as well as behind strikers. Despite his small frame, he has also shown a great ability to head the ball, with some of his most impressive goals coming in the air.*

LEFT: *Xabi Alonso, joined Liverpool from Real Sociedad by their recently-installed manager Rafael Benitez, for a fee of £10.5m. The midfielder is a dangerous free kick specialist.*

SWEDEN

STRONG AT the back, but also dangerous going forward – Sweden will be a threat at the World Cup. Under coach Lars Lagerback, who took full control when co-coach Tommy Soderberg took over the Under-21 side in 2004, the Swedes qualified comfortably as one of the best group runners-up. The main reason for that success was the eight goals from striker Zlatan Ibrahimovic who showed just why Juventus paid around £13m for his services two seasons ago.

The tall 24-year-old has struck up a formidable partnership with Henrik Larsson who came out of international retirement to play in the Euro2004 tournament and who has been on fire ever since. The front two are ably assisted by an attack-minded midfield, most notably Arsenal's Fredrik Ljungberg who himself netted seven goals in qualifying.

Sweden do not give much away at the other end, with Olof Mellberg and Teddy Lucic providing a powerful and no-nonsense barrier in front of goalkeeper Andreas Isaksson. Four years ago the Scandinavians topped a World Cup Finals group that included Argentina and England and looked set to go a long way, only to be beaten by Senegal in the first knock-out round.

Lagerback may expect the current crop to go at least as far, and perhaps even further – although they are unlikely to match their place in the 1958 Final or the third-placed finish they achieved in 1994.

SWEDEN

FOUNDED	1904
AFFILIATED	1904
WC PARTICIPATIONS	10 (1934, 1938, 1950, 1958, 1970, 1974, 1978, 1990, 1994, 2002)
WC RECORD	Runners-up 1958
CONTINENTAL TITLES	None
FIFA WORLD RANKING	14
COACH	Lars Lagerback
ROUTE TO GERMANY	Runners Up European Group 8
BOOKMAKERS ODDS	33-1

PLAYERS TO WATCH

TOP LEFT: *Fredrik Ljungberg joined Arsenal in 1998 after playing for Halmstads BK in Sweden he is also an underwear model for Calvin Klein with a particular following from the gay community.*

TOP RIGHT: *Zlatan Ibrahimovic, striker currently playing for Juventus in Italian Serie A. He started playing football at the age of 10. His initial club was FBK Balkan and consisted mostly of immigrants from the Rosengård neighbourhood. Later, Ibrahimović started professional football with the Swedish club Malmö FF in the 1999-2000 season.*

LEFT: *Henrik Larsson, a prolific goal scorer having completed seven very successful years with Celtic in Glasgow, Scotland, after the end of the 2003/04 season he signed a one year contract with an option for a second year for Spanish giants Barcelona. Despite having missed the majority of season 2004/2005 through injury, the option to play in season 2005/2006 was extended and accepted.*

SWITZERLAND

SWITZERLAND PRODUCED perhaps the most impressive - and also dramatic - performances to reach the Finals. Drawn in a qualifying group that included mighty France, powerful Republic of Ireland and the emerging Israelis, the Swiss were given little chance of making it to Germany. However, thanks mainly to the seven goals from Rennes striker Alex Frei, they were within one goal of finishing top before eventually being forced to settle for a place in the play-offs.

Even then they were rated underdogs against Turkey, but won 2-0 at home before going through on away goals despite a ferocious 4-2 defeat in Istanbul that was marred by fighting between the players after the final whistle.

Qualification came largely without the influential Yakin brothers, Murat and Hakan, due to injuries, and coach Koebi Kuhn will hope they will both be fully fit by the time the action gets underway this summer. However, in wingers Johann Vogel and Raphael Wicky, Switzerland have found two more dangermen going forward.

Frei will carry the weight of expectations in the Finals themselves again, but 20-year-old sensation Johan Vonlanthen is ready to make a big impact having become the youngest ever goalscorer in the European Championships two years ago.

SWITZERLAND

FOUNDED	1895
AFFILIATED	1904
WC PARTICIPATIONS	7 (1934, 1938, 1950, 1954, 1962, 1966, 1994)
WC RECORD	Quarter-finals 1934, 1938, 1954
CONTINENTAL TITLES	None
FIFA WORLD RANKING	36
COACH	Kobi Kuhn
ROUTE TO GERMANY	European Play Off Winners
BOOKMAKERS ODDS	125-1

PLAYERS TO WATCH

TOP LEFT: *Alexander Frei, currently playing for Stade Rennais FC in the Ligue 1, as a striker, he was the highest goalscorer in the league for the 2004/05 season with 20 goals, and was named Swiss footballer of the year the same season.*

TOP RIGHT: *Johann Vogel, currently plays for AC Milan, and is the captain of the Switzerland national football team.*

LEFT: *Philippe Senderos, currently playing for Arsenal F.C. as a defender.*

TOGO

TOGO ARE yet another west African nation making their debut at the World Cup Finals. Their qualification was perhaps the biggest shock of all, as they topped a group that included Senegal – the team that caused such a sensation at the 2002 tournament when they beat reigning champions France. Even more surprising was the fact Togo had actually lost their first group game to Zambia, but then remained unbeaten and booked their place in Germany with a nail-biting 3-2 win over Congo in their final fixture as they battled back from 2-1 down.

Their success has been built on the goals of Monaco striker Emmanuel Adebayor who netted 11 times in qualifying. He was actually born in Nigeria, with fellow striker Adekamni Olufade also turning his back on the Super Eagles to represent Togo's Hawks instead. In an attack-minded formation, Abdel Coubadja is also a dangerman in front of goal, while a defence marshalled by Dare Nibombe and Jean-Paul Abalo conceded just eight goals on the road to the Finals.

Togo, who have swept into the top 50 in the world over the past year, will be led by coach Stephen Keshi, another Nigerian who represented his homeland at the 1994 World Cup Finals.

TOGO

FOUNDED	1960
AFFILIATED	1962
WC PARTICIPATIONS	None
WC RECORD	No previous finals
CONTINENTAL TITLES	None
FIFA WORLD RANKING	56
COACH	Stephane Queshi (Nigeria)
ROUTE TO GERMANY	Winners African Group 1
BOOKMAKERS ODDS	400-1

PLAYERS TO WATCH

TOP LEFT: *Emmanuel Adebayor, currently plays for AS Monaco. He joined the club from FC Metz in 2003.*

TOP RIGHT: *Abdel Coubadja, striker who plays for Sochaux in France.*

LEFT: *Kossi Agassa, goalkeeper for French team FC Metz.*

TRINIDAD & TOBAGO

SUCH WAS the delight when Trinidad and Tobago qualified for the World Cup that the Government declared the following day a national holiday. That jubilant moment came after a nail-biting 2-1 play-off victory over Bahrain that put the Soca Warriors into their first ever major tournament. It capped a remarkable turnaround for Trinidad given the fact they had finished rock bottom in the final qualifying stage for the 2002 World Cup behind Jamaica and Honduras.

This time around, thanks to veterans such as Dwight Yorke and Russell Latapy, they finished fourth in the group and then saw off Bahrain over two legs to book their place in Germany. They will be managed by cigar-smoking Leo Beenhakker who has a wealth of experience after spells in charge of Ajax, Real Madrid and the Dutch national team.

However, he will have to work hard to ensure Trinidad's joy at reaching the World Cup party is not spoiled by some heavy defeats. Players such as Clayton Ince, Ian Cox, Dennis Lawrence, Carlos Edwards, Chris Birchall and Stern John will no doubt give everything, but they can be more regularly found playing in the lower divisions in England and will be making a big step up in class in Germany.

TRINIDAD & TOBAGO

FOUNDED	1908
AFFILIATED	1963
WC PARTICIPATIONS	None
WC RECORD	No previous final
CONTINENTAL TITLES	None
FIFA WORLD RANKING	51
COACH	Leo Beenhakker (Holland)
ROUTE TO GERMANY	Winners Asian and North/Central and Caribbean Play Offs
BOOKMAKERS ODDS	750-1

PLAYERS TO WATCH

TOP LEFT: *Stern John, who currently plays for Derby County F.C. of the Football League Championship on loan from Coventry City F.C. He is a centre forward.*

TOP RIGHT: *Dwight Yorke, currently plays for Sydney FC in the Australian A-League; he has previously played for Aston Villa, Manchester United, Blackburn Rovers, and Birmingham City.*

LEFT: *Russell Latapy, currently plays for Falkirk in the Scottish Premier League, where he is also a first team coach. He has previously played for Hibernian, Rangers, Dundee United, FC Porto, and Boavista.*

TUNISIA

TUNISIA GO into their fourth World Cup full of confidence after topping a difficult qualifying group that included north African rivals Morocco. On top of that, the Tunisians top-scored over the entire continent with 25 goals from their 10 games, thanks largely to star striker Santos. The Brazilian-born forward took Tunisian nationality back in 2004 and netted six times on the road to Germany, highlighting the reason why Toulouse swooped to take him from Sochaux in 2005.

As the Eagles of Carthage – as the Tunisians are known – have progressed, so their players have been targeted by big clubs across Europe. Defender Radhi Jaidi has been impressive since joining Bolton, while full-back Hatem Trabelsi has increasingly been linked with a move from Ajax to Arsenal.

The squad proved their collective ability in 2004 when they won the African Nations Cup on home soil and coach Roger Lemerre will be hoping their form continues on the world stage. Lemerre himself has more reason than most to want to do well after his reputation took a battering at the tournament four years ago. He was dismissed as France coach after a dreadful World Cup that saw Les Blues fail to score a single goal.

TUNISIA

FOUNDED	1956
AFFILIATED	1960
WC PARTICIPATIONS	1978, 1998, 2002
WC RECORD	Group Stage 1978, 1998, 2002
CONTINENTAL TITLES	None
FIFA WORLD RANKING	28
COACH	Roger Lemerre (France)
ROUTE TO GERMANY	African Group 5 Winners
BOOKMAKERS ODDS	300-1

PLAYERS TO WATCH

TOP LEFT: *Silva Dos Santos, the Brazilian born attacker plays for French second division side FC Sochaux.*

TOP RIGHT: *Hatem Trabelsi, the Ajax defender the ever-dependable right-back is a vital cog in the Tunisian team and is blessed with athleticism, pace and a sublime technique for a defender.*

LEFT: *Radhi Jaidi, the defender, arrived at Bolton Wanderers from Esperance in the summer of 2004.*

UKRAINE

ANDREI SHEVCHENKO will undoubtedly grab the spotlight for Ukraine, but opponents would do well not to concentrate solely on the AC Milan star. Star Shevchenko was top scorer in qualifying with six goals, but with Andrei Vorobey and Andrei Voronin employed in an attack-minded formation, Ukraine were the first team to book their place in the Finals behind hosts Germany. That was due to an impressive campaign that saw them lose just one game - and that after they had already qualified - in a group that included Turkey, Denmark and European Champions Greece. It all means that Ukraine, despite being unseeded, will pose some serious problems and have a great chance of reaching the knock-out stages, despite this being their debut in the World Cup. They almost made it to the Finals back in 1998 and 2002, but suffered the agony of defeat in the play-offs against Croatia and Germany respectively. And coach Oleg Blokhin, who was European Footballer of the Year in 1975, is sure to enjoy the occasion more than most after he was on the verge of quitting the job in March 2005. He actually submitted a resignation letter following rows about his dual-role as an MP in the Ukrainian parliament, before a court decision allowed him to remain as coach as long as he is not paid for the job.

UKRAINE

FOUNDED	1991
AFFILIATED	1992
WC PARTICIPATIONS	None
WC RECORD	No previous finals
CONTINENTAL TITLES	None
FIFA WORLD RANKING	40
COACH	Oleg Blokhin
ROUTE TO GERMANY	Winners European Group 2
BOOKMAKERS ODDS	50-1

PLAYERS TO WATCH

TOP LEFT: *Andrei Shevchenko, AC Milans deadly assasin was named the European Footballer of the Year in 2004. Shevchenko has represented Ukraine in 63 matches and scored 28 international goals.*

TOP RIGHT: *Andrei Voronin has been an attacker with Bayer 04 Leverkusen since 2004. His previous clubs include Chornomorets Odessa, Borussia Mönchengladbach, FSV Mainz 05 and 1. FC Köln.*

LEFT: *Oleh Husyev, striker, plays for Dynamo Kiev.*

USA

FOOTBALL MAY well still be a minority male sport in the USA, but their national team will be making its fifth consecutive World Cup appearance in Germany. Having made it through the quarter-finals four years ago, expectations are high, but they qualified for this tournament with three games to spare and have a powerful blend of youth and experience. The old heads include a trio of decent goalkeepers in Kasey Keller, Tim Howard and Marcus Hahnemann, skipper Claudio Reyna and striker Brian McBride. However, they have been joined by energetic talent such as Landon Donovan, DaMarcus Beasley and Bobby Convey who add a spark to the style of play.

Most interesting of all could be the highly rated Freddy Adu who is already being trailed by the likes of Chelsea and Manchester United despite being just 17-years-old. Coach Bruce Arena could have a difficult dilemma over whether to throw such an inexperienced, yet obviously talented, player such as Adu into the World Cup - but some are already saying if he gets his chance he could make the same impact as Pele did at the same age in Sweden in 1958.

USA are unlikely to repeat Brazil's feat of winning that tournament, but they can expect to be extremely competitive again in Germany.

USA

FOUNDED	1913
AFFILIATED	1913
WC PARTICIPATIONS	7 (1930, 1934, 1950, 1990, 1994, 1998, 2002)
WC RECORD	Semi-finals 1930
CONTINENTAL TITLES	Gold Cup (1991, 2002), Pan American champions (1991)
FIFA WORLD RANKING	8
COACH	Bruce Arena
ROUTE TO GERMANY	Winners CONCACAF Final Group
BOOKMAKERS ODDS	80-1

PLAYERS TO WATCH

TOP LEFT: *Freddy Adu, a Ghanaian born American, has gained fame for his prodigious soccer talent. At the age of 14, he signed a professional contract with the D.C. United Major League Soccer (MLS) team on November 18, 2003. Expect him to shine at the World Cup and playing in Europe next season with a host of the major clubs wanting his services.*

TOP RIGHT: *Brian McBride, currently plays forward for Fulham.*

LEFT: *DaMarcus Beasley, prolific winger moved to Europe in 2004 to play for the Dutch team PSV Eindhoven.*

GERMANY 2006

BERLIN

POPULATION	3.39 million
STADIUM	Olympiastadion
PROJECT	Reconstruction
INVESTMENT	€242m
GROSS CAPACITY	74,220
TOTAL SEATING CAPACITY	66,021
PURCHASABLE TICKET CAPACITY	Group stage: 56,358, Quarter-finals: 56,316, Final: 55,562

COLOGNE

POPULATION	1 Million
STADIUM	FIFA World Cup Stadium Cologne
PROJECT	Reconstruction
INVESTMENT	€110m
GROSS CAPACITY	46,120
TOTAL SEATING CAPACITY	40,590
PURCHASABLE TICKET CAPACITY	Group stage: 35,926, Round of sixteen: 35,580

VENUES

DORTMUND

POPULATION	590,000
STADIUM	Westfalenstadion
PROJECT	Reconstruction
INVESTMENT	€40m plus €5.5m modernisation programme
GROSS CAPACITY	65,982
TOTAL SEATING CAPACITY	60,285
PURCHASABLE TICKET CAPACITY	Group stage: 50,768, Round of sixteen: 50,276, Semi-finals: 49,876

FRANKFURT

POPULATION	650,000
STADIUM	Waldstadion
PROJECT	New stadium
INVESTMENT	€126m
GROSS CAPACITY	48,132
TOTAL SEATING CAPACITY	43,324
PURCHASABLE TICKET CAPACITY	Group stage: 38,437, Quarter-finals: 37,925

GERMANY 2006

GELSENKIRCHEN

POPULATION	278,000
STADIUM	FIFA World Cup Stadium Gelsenkirchen
PROJECT	New stadium
INVESTMENT	€191m
GROSS CAPACITY	53,804
TOTAL SEATING CAPACITY	48,426
PURCHASABLE TICKET CAPACITY	Group stage: 43,920, Quarter-finals: 43,574

HAMBURG

POPULATION	1.7 million
STADIUM	FIFA World Cup Stadium Hamburg
PROJECT	New stadium
INVESTMENT	€97m
GROSS CAPACITY	51,055
TOTAL SEATING CAPACITY	45,442
PURCHASABLE TICKET CAPACITY	Group stage: 40,918, Quarter-finals: 40,226

VENUES

HANOVER

POPULATION	525,000
STADIUM	FIFA World Cup Stadium Hanover
PROJECT	Reconstruction
INVESTMENT	€64m
GROSS CAPACITY	44,652
TOTAL SEATING CAPACITY	39,297
PURCHASABLE TICKET CAPACITY	Group stage: 34,311, Round of sixteen: 33,965

KAISERSLAUTERN

POPULATION	100,000
STADIUM	Fritz-Walter-Stadion
PROJECT	Extension
INVESTMENT	€48.3m
GROSS CAPACITY	41,170
TOTAL SEATING CAPACITY	41,513
PURCHASABLE TICKET CAPACITY	Group stage: 37,084, Round of sixteen: 36,392

GERMANY 2006

LEIPZIG

POPULATION	494,000
STADIUM	Zentralstadion
PROJECT	New stadium
INVESTMENT	€90.6m
GROSS CAPACITY	44,199
TOTAL SEATING CAPACITY	38,898
PURCHASABLE TICKET CAPACITY	Group stage: 34,384, Round of sixteen: 34,038

MUNICH

POPULATION	1.3 million
STADIUM	FIFA World Cup Stadium Munich
PROJECT	New stadium
INVESTMENT	approx €280m
GROSS CAPACITY	66,016
TOTAL SEATING CAPACITY	59,416
PURCHASABLE TICKET CAPACITY	Group stage: 52,782, Round of sixteen: 52,636, Semi-finals: 52,090

VENUES

NUREMBERG

POPULATION	490,000
STADIUM	Frankenstadion
PROJECT	Reconstruction
INVESTMENT	€56m
GROSS CAPACITY	41,926
TOTAL SEATING CAPACITY	36,898
PURCHASABLE TICKET CAPACITY	Group stage: 32,341, Round of sixteen: 31,995

STUTTGART

POPULATION	590,000
STADIUM	Gottlieb-Daimler-Stadion
PROJECT	Modernisation
INVESTMENT	€51.5 m
GROSS CAPACITY	53,200
TOTAL SEATING CAPACITY	47,757
PURCHASABLE TICKET CAPACITY	Group stage: 39,030, Round of sixteen: 38,884, Third place match: 38,538

INDEX